China's Peril and Promise

- An Advanced Reader -

Vocabulary
and
Grammar Notes

China's Peril and Promise

中國的危機與希望

- An Advanced Reader -

Vocabulary
and
Grammar Notes

周質平　　王學東　　楊 玖
Chih-p'ing Chou　Xuedong Wang　Joanne Chiang

Princeton University Press
Princeton, New Jersey

Copyright © 1996 by Princeton University Press
Published by Princeton University Press, 41 William Street,
Princeton, New Jersey 08540
In the United Kingdom: Princeton University Press,
Chichester, West Sussex

All Rights Reserved

ISBN 0-691-02884-2

The publisher would like to acknowledge the authors of these volumes for providing the camera-ready
copy from which these books were printed

Princeton University Press books are printed on acid-free paper and meet the
guidelines for permanence and durability of the Committee on Production
Guidelines for Book Longevity of the Council on Library Resources

Printed in the United States of America by Princeton Academic Press

1 3 5 7 9 10 8 6 4 2

目　　录

China's Peril and Promise

- An Advanced Reader -

Vocabulary
and
Grammar Notes

（一）

立　論

立論	立论	lìlùn	to take a stand
講堂	讲堂	jiǎngtáng	lecture hall, classroom
請教	请教	qǐngjiào	to ask for advice, to consult
眼鏡	眼镜	yǎnjìng	glasses, spectacles
圈		quān	circle, ring
斜		xié	slanting, inclined
射出		shèchū	to emit (light, heat, etc.), to shoot
眼光		yǎnguāng	eye, glance
闔家	合家	héjiā	the whole family
透頂	透顶	tòudǐng	thoroughly, in the extreme
滿月	满月	mǎnyuè	a baby's completion of its first month of life
兆頭	兆头	zhàotou	sign, omen
發財	发财	fācái	to get rich, to make a fortune
番		fān	measure word for actions
恭維	恭维	gōngwei	flatter, compliment

合力		hélì	join forces, combine efforts
痛打		tòngdǎ	a sound beating, a severe thrashing
必然		bìrán	inevitable, certain
說謊	说谎	shuōhuǎng	to lie
好報	好报	hǎobào	retribution, reward
遭打		zāodǎ	to be beaten
瞧		qiáo	to look, to see

立 论

词语例句

一. 向...请教   to ask advice from

※ 我梦见自己在小学校的讲堂上预备作文，向老师请教立论的方法。

1. 这个问题我非向你请教不可。

2. 我之所以给他打电话，是想向他请教怎么解决这个难题。

二. ...透顶   to be extremely adj.

                                  （often undesirable）

※ 一家人家生了一个男孩，阖家高兴透顶了。

1. 我听了他的话，简直失望透顶。

2. 你真是糊涂透顶，你怎么能对他说这个儿子将来是要死的呢!

三. 既不...，也不...   neither ... nor ...

※ 我愿意既不谎人，也不遭打。

1. 他既不聪明，也不漂亮。

2. 他既没感谢我，也没恭维我。

（二）

聰明人和傻子和奴才

傻子	傻子	shǎzi	fool
奴才		núcai	slave, serf, bondman
尋	寻	xún	to look for, to search for
訴苦	诉苦	sùkǔ	to vent one's grievances
悲哀		bēiāi	sorrowful
連	连	lián	in succession, one after another
眼角		yǎnjiǎo	corner of the eye
未必		wèibì	不一定
高粱		gāoliang	sorghum
慘然	惨然	cǎnrán	sadly, sorrowfully
晝夜	昼夜	zhòuyè	day and night, round the clock
擔	担	dān	to carry on a shoulder pole
磨		mó	to grind
晴		qíng	clear, sunny
衣裳		yīshang	衣服

張	张	zhāng	to open, to unfurl
傘	伞	sǎn	umbrella
汽爐	汽炉	qìlú	gas stove
扇		shàn	fan
煨		wēi	to cook over a slow fire, to simmer
銀耳	银耳	yín'ěr	a kind of semi-transparent white fungus believed to be highly nutritious
耍錢	耍钱	shuǎqián	to gamble (archaic), 賭博
頭錢	头钱	tóuqian	fee paid to the host and organizer of a gambling party
没份	没份	méifèn	to not have a share
挨		ái	to suffer (hunger, beating, etc.)
皮鞭		píbiān	leather-thonged whip
嘆息	叹息	tànxī	to sigh
眼圈		yǎnquān	rim of the eye
發紅	发红	fāhóng	to turn red
敷衍		fūyǎn	to act in a perfunctory manner
但願	但愿	dànyuàn	if only, I wish
冤苦		yuānkǔ	wrongful treatment

安慰		ānwèi	to comfort; comfort
舒坦		shūtan	to be at ease, to feel comfortable
可見	可见	kějiàn	it is thus clear that
天理		tiānlǐ	justice
滅絕	灭绝	mièjué	to become extinct
不平		bùpíng	indignant, resentful
猪窠		zhūkē	pigsty
主人		zhǔrén	master
叭兒狗		bā'ergǒu	Pekinese dog (a breed of dog)
混帳	混帐	hùnzhàng	son of a bitch
吃驚	吃惊	chījīng	to be startled, to be shocked
陰	阴	yīn	dark, gloomy
臭蟲	臭虫	chòuchóng	bedbug
穢氣	秽气	huìqì	stench
衝	冲	chòng	to direct (one's attack, etc.) toward
動手	动手	dòngshǒu	to start work
砸		zá	to smash

泥牆	泥墙	níqiáng	clay wall
罵	骂	mà	to scold
管他呢		guǎn tā ne	Who cares!
强盗		qiángdào	bandit
毀		huǐ	to destroy, to ruin
窟窿		kūlong	hole
團團的	团团的	tuántuánde	round and round
打滾		dǎgǔn	to roll about
趕走	赶走	gǎnzǒu	to drive away
恭敬		gōngjìng	respectful
得勝	得胜	déshèng	triumphant
誇獎	夸奖	kuājiǎng	to praise, to commend
慰問	慰问	wèiwèn	to convey greetings to, to extend one's regards to
有功		yǒugōng	to have rendered great service
先見之明	先见之明	xiān jiàn zhī míng	foresight

聪明人和傻子和奴才
词语例句

一．不过是   merely, no more than

※ 奴才总不过是寻人诉苦。

1．他不过是开开玩笑，并不认真。

2．考试不过是测验自己懂了多少，不必紧张。

二．未必   not necessarily

※ 我吃的是一天未必有一餐，这一餐又不过是高粱皮。

1．他虽然从事这个行业多年，未必喜爱这个工作。

2．成绩好的学生未必是最聪明的学生。

三．尚且   moreover（＝而且）；even（＝甚至）

※ 这一餐不过是高粱皮，连猪狗都不要吃的，尚且只有一小碗。

1．我的经验不足，尚且时间不够，恐怕没法子做好这个工作。

2．老师尚且不能全懂，学生当然觉得非常困难。

四．可见   thus it is clear that

※ 我得了你的同情和安慰，已经舒坦得不少了，可见天理没有灭绝。

1．失业率不断上升，可见经济还在衰退。

2．他的成绩迅速进步，可见他最近很用功。

五．A 比 B 还不如   A is even worse than B

※ 我住得简直比猪窠还不如。

1．我的中文不太好，他的简直比我的还不如。

2．人人都说纽约的交通混乱，可是我看波士顿简直比纽约还不如。

六. ...得真可以   to be awfully adj.

　※ 屋子里满是臭虫，睡下去就咬得真可以。

　1. 那个孩子笨得真可以，学了三天还不会写自己的名字。

　2. 屋子里乱得真可以，简直像小偷来过似的。

七. ...在内   to include, to be included

　※ 这一天来了许多慰问的人，聪明人也在内。

　1. 我们讨论了许多题目，张先生昨天谈到的问题也在内。

　2. 连房租在内，这个月一共花费了三千块钱。

(三)

中國人，你爲甚麼不生氣

微笑		wēixiào	to smile
檢驗	检验	jiǎnyàn	to examine; to test
合格		hégé	up to standard; qualified
廠商	厂商	chǎngshāng	manufacturer and business firms
揭露		jiēlù	to expose; to unmask
生意人		shēngyìrén	businessman
吃飯	吃饭	chīfàn	to make a living(metaphor)
惡心	恶心	ěxīn	to feel sick; nauseated
憤怒	愤怒	fènnù	to be angry; indignant
對象	对象	duìxiàng	target; object
女士		nǚshì	lady
懦弱		nuòruò	weak; cowardly
自私		zìsī	selfish
包德甫		Bāodéfǔ	Chinese name of Fox Butterfield
苦海餘生	苦海余生	Kǔhǎiyúshēng	*China, Alive in the Bitter Sea* by Fox Butterfield

10

原本		yuánběn	the original text; original manuscript
撞傷	撞伤	zhuàngshāng	to injure by hitting (usually with a vehicle or large object)
過路	过路	guòlù	to pass by
受傷	受伤	shòushāng	to be injured
譴責	谴责	qiǎnzé	to condemn; to blame
肇事		zhàoshì	to make trouble
人情味		rénqíngwèi	warmth and friendliness; quality of being humane
自詡	自诩	zìxǔ	to brag; to praise oneself
發覺	发觉	fājué	to find; to discover
描述		miáoshù	to describe
隨地	随地	suídì	到處
常態	常态	chángtài	normal state
生存		shēngcún	to survive
蟑螂		zhāngláng	cockroaches
怕事		pàshì	to be afraid of getting into trouble; overly cautious
寧可	宁可	nìngkě	would rather
假寐		jiǎmèi	to pretend to be asleep

攤販	摊贩	tānfàn	street vendor
占據	占据	zhànjù	to occupy
騎樓	骑楼	qílóu	the part of a building which overhangs the sidewalk
走廊		zǒuláng	corridor; hallway
垢上		gòushàng	to dirty; to cover with filth; to grease
層	层	céng	layer
厚		hòu	thick
油污		yóuwū	greasy dirt
腐臭		fǔchòu	putrid-/rotten-smelling
牆腳	墙脚	qiángjiǎo	the base of a wall
猜拳		cāiquán	to play a Chinese drinking game
作樂	作乐	zuòlè	to make merry, to have fun
鷄犬不寧	鸡犬不宁	jī quǎn bù níng	even chickens and dogs are not left in peace; extremely noisy
滾蛋		gǔndàn	Scram! Get lost!
流氓		liúmáng	hoodlums
相熟		xiāngshú	to be well-acquainted or familiar with
若		ruò	如果，要是

曝光	暴光	bàoguāng	to expose
惹禍上門	惹祸上门	rě huò shàng mén	to bring trouble to oneself
忍		rěn	to tolerate; to put up with; to endure
反正		fǎnzhèng	anyway, in any case
忍耐		rěnnài	self-restraint; endurance; patience
聳肩	耸肩	sǒngjiān	to shrug one's shoulders
法治		fǎzhì	to rule by law
軌道	轨道	guǐdào	following regulations and conventions (extended meaning); track
受折磨		shòu zhémó	to suffer; to be tormented
叉腰		chāyāo	to place arms akimbo
勾結	勾结	gōujié	to gang up with
怒火		nùhuǒ	fury
蕭清	肃清	sùqīng	to enforce (discipline)
紀律	纪律	jìlǜ	discipline; laws and regulations
畏縮	畏缩	wèisuō	to recoil from; to flinch from
淡水河		Dànshuǐhé	Dan-Shui River
河畔		hépàn	riverbank

欣賞	欣賞	xīnshǎng	to enjoy
落日		luòrì	the setting sun
住家		zhùjiā	resident
整籠	整笼	zhěnglóng	a full basket
惡臭	惡臭	èchòu	foul smelling
垃圾		lājī	garbage
倒		dào	to dump; to pour
排泄		páixiè	drainage
管		guǎn	pipe
通		tōng	to lead to
漲	涨	zhǎng	to rise; to swell
污穢	污秽	wūhuì	dirty; filthy
逼		bī	to press up to
呼吸	呼吸	hūxī	breath
勇氣	勇气	yǒngqì	courage
丟		diū	to throw
瓶		píng	bottle

釣魚	钓鱼	diàoyú	to fish
佈滿	布满	bùmǎn	to be covered with
癌		ái	cancer
細胞	细胞	xìbāo	cell
假裝		jiǎzhuāng	to pretend
化解		huàjiě	to melt; to dissolve; to be biodegradable
魚竿	鱼竿	yúgān	fishing rod
一整列		yīzhěngliè	a whole train of
停滯	停滞	tíngzhì	to stop; to stagnate
阻塞		zǔsè	traffic jam; blockage; obstruction
方向盤	方向盘	fāngxiàngpán	steering wheel
嘆氣	叹气	tànqì	to sigh
無奈	无奈	wúnài	沒法子
理論	理论	lǐlùn	講道理
扁鑽	扁钻	biǎnzuàn	flat chisel
阻礙	阻碍	zǔ'ài	to block
有種	有种	yǒuzhǒng	to have guts

果斷	果断	guǒduàn	resolutely; with determination
不齒	不齿	bùchǐ	to hold in contempt; to despise
行爲	行为	xíngwéi	behavior
郊區	郊区	jiāoqū	suburb
刺鼻		cìbí	to irritate the nose
化學品	化学品	huàxuépǐn	chemicals
燃燒	燃烧	ránshāo	burning
海灘	海滩	hǎitān	beach
廢料	废料	fèiliào	waste
股		gǔ	measure word for things such as water, streams, and steam
染		rǎn	to dye
奇異	奇异	qíyì	strange
灣	湾	wān	bay
焚燒	焚烧	fénshāo	to burn
電纜	电缆	diànlǎn	cable
缺少		quēshǎo	沒有 ; to lack
腦子	脑子	nǎozi	brain

16

嬰兒	嬰儿	yīng'ér	infant
明亮		míngliàng	bright
嗓音		sǎngyīn	voice
稚嫩		zhìnèn	young and delicate
臉頰	脸颊	liǎnjiá	cheeks
游泳		yóuyǒng	to swim
血管		xuèguǎn	blood vessel
毒素		dúsù	poison
手臂		shǒubì	arm
温柔		wēnróu	tender and gentle
捧		pěng	to hold in both hands
哭泣		kūqì	to cry
頻頻	频频	pínpín	repeatedly; incessantly
叮嚀	叮咛	dīngníng	to urge; to warn again and again
飲料	饮料	yǐnliào	drink, beverage
瓶裝		píngzhuāng	bottled
寶島	宝岛	bǎodǎo	precious island

17

名譽	名誉	míngyù	reputation; fame
其次		qícì	secondary; next (in importance)
交大		Jiāodà	交通大學
食物中毒		shíwù zhòngdú	food poisoning
值錢	值钱	zhíqián	valuable
總算	总算	zǒngsuàn	finally; at last
消費者	消费者	xiāofèizhě	consumer
團體	团体	tuántǐ	organization
茅坑		máokēng	latrine pit
拉屎		lāshǐ	to defecate
占着茅坑不拉屎		zhànzhe máo kēng bù lāshǐ	to occupy a position without fulfilling its duties
衛生署	卫生署	wèishēngshǔ	Sanitation Department
説客	说客	shuōkè	a persuasive talker; lobbyist
立法委員	立法委员	lìfǎwěiyuán	member of the legislature
扼殺	扼杀	èshā	to strangle in the cradle
椿	桩	zhuāng	measure word for events
良心		liángxīn	conscience

躲		duǒ	to hide
角落		jiǎoluò	corner
沉默		chénmò	silent, quiet
退讓	退让	tuìràng	to give in
破落		pòluò	poor and broken down
大雜院	大杂院	dàzáyuàn	a compound occupied by many households
烏烟瘴氣	乌烟瘴气	wūyān zhàngqì	foul atmosphere
爛腸子	烂肠子	lànchángzi	rotten animal intestines
疼愛	疼爱	téng'ài	to be very fond of; to dote on
娃娃		wáwa	baby
孕婦	孕妇	yùnfù	pregnant women
懷胎	怀胎	huáitāi	to be pregnant
滴		dī	drip
純淨	纯净	chúnjìng	pure and clean
沙拉油		shālāyóu	cooking oil
瞎		xiā	to be blind
殺猪的	杀猪的	shāzhūde	butcher

不够資格	不够资格	búgòuzīgé	not qualified
犧牲者	牺牲者	xīshēngzhě	sacrificial victims
受害人		shòuhàirén	victim
公僕	公仆	gōngpú	public servant
環保局	环保局	huánbǎojú	Environmental Protection Bureau

中国人，你为什么不生气?
词语例句

一． 倒不是　A，而是　B　　　　　　　　　　　　it is not A, but B

※ 我生气的对象倒不是这位女士，而是台湾一千八百万懦弱自私的
中国人。

1． 那个中国人在家中说的倒不是中国话，而是日本话。

2． 他说中国的传统观念太保守，我看保守的倒不是传统的中国观念，
而是现代的中国人。

二． 以…自诩　　　　　　　　　　　　　　to praise oneself, to brag

※ 中国人以有人情味自诩。

1． 中国人常以悠久的历史自诩。

2． 美国人以其民主自由自诩。

三． 只要…，宁可…　　　So long as …,（one）would rather …

※ 只要不杀到他床上去，他宁可闭着眼假寐。

1． 只要你不反对，我宁可用我自己的方法来做，虽然经理可能不喜
欢这个方法。

2． 只要他的病能治好，我宁可用尽所有的钱。

四． 在于　　　　　　　　　　　　　　　　　　　　　to lie in

※ 问题不在于他带不带扁钻，问题在于你们没有种!

1． 美国的犯罪率高，原因不在于贫穷，而在于道德败坏。

2． 解决社会问题不在于政府的倡导，而在于教育。

五． 其次　　　　　　　　　　　　　　　　to be the secondary

※ 宝岛的名誉还是其次，最重要的是我们的健康。

1． 提到找工作，赚多少钱是其次，最重要的是你有没有兴趣。

2. 这门课功课重不重是其次，有用没有用才是最重要的。

六. 好不容易　　　　　　　to have a hard time （doing something）, with great difficulty

※ 好不容易有人组织了一个消费者团体，却又有人要扼杀这个组织。

1. 我好不容易说服了他，你却又来找麻烦。

2. 他好不容易才克服了困难，我们应当多鼓励他。

（四）

風　箏

風箏	风筝	fēngzheng	kite
冬季		dōngjì	winter
積雪	积雪	jīxuě	deposits of snow
禿		tū	bald, bare
椏叉	丫叉	yāchā	to branch out
晴朗		qínglǎng	clear and bright
浮動	浮动	fúdòng	to float
驚異	惊异	jīngyì	astonishment
悲哀		bēi'āi	sadness
故鄉	故乡	gùxiāng	hometown
時節	时节	shíjié	time, season
倘		tǎng	if
沙沙		shāshā	whirring or buzzing sound
風輪	风轮	fēnglún	pinwheel
仰頭	仰头	yǎngtóu	to raise one's head

淡墨色		dànmòsè	light ink color
蟹		xiè	crab
嫩		nèn	light; tender
蜈蚣		wúgōng	centipede
寂寞		jìmò	lonely, solitary
瓦片		wǎpiàn	tile
放風箏	放风筝	fàng fēngzheng	to fly a kite
伶仃		língdīng	lonely, solitary
顯出	显出	xiǎnchū	to exhibit, to show
憔悴		qiáocuì	haggard, worn out
模樣	模样	móyàng	appearance
楊柳	杨柳	yángliǔ	willow
發芽	发芽	fāyá	to bud
山桃		shāntáo	wild peach
吐蕾		tǔlěi	to sprout buds
點綴	点缀	diǎnzhuì	decoration
照應	照应	zhàoyìng	to correspond; to match

温和		wēnhé	warmth
嚴冬	严冬	yándōng	severe winter
蕭殺	肃杀	sùshā	austerity, severeness
久經訣別	久经诀别	jiǔ jīng jué bié	long-departed
久經逝去	久经逝去	jiǔ jīng shì qù	long-past
盪漾	荡漾	dàngyàng	to wave, to ripple
嫌惡	嫌恶	xiánwù	to be disgusted by, to despise
没出息		méi chūxi	good-for-nothing
玩藝兒	玩艺儿	wányìr	plaything, toy
相反		xiāngfǎn	opposite
不堪		bùkān	to be unable to bear
呆		dāi	blankly
出神		chūshén	to be engrossed in meditation
驚呼	惊呼	jīnghū	to yell in surprise
纏繞	缠绕	chánrào	entanglement
跳躍	跳跃	tiàoyuè	to jump
笑柄		xiàobǐng	butt of a joke; laughing stock

可鄙		kěbǐ	contemptible
枯竹		kūzhú	dried bamboo
恍然大悟		huǎng rán dà wù	to suddenly realize
堆積	堆积	duījī	to store up
雜物	杂物	záwù	odds and ends
果然		guǒrán	as expected
塵封的		chénfēngde	dust-covered
什物		shíwù	雜物
驚惶	惊惶	jīnghuáng	alarmed
失了色		shīlesè	to become pale because of fear
瑟縮		sèsuō	to tremble and shrink back
蝴蝶		húdié	butterfly
骨		gǔ	frame, skeleton
糊		hú	to paste
裝飾	装饰	zhuāngshì	to beautify, to decorate
破獲	破获	pòhuò	to uncover, to reveal
秘密		mìmì	secret

滿足	满足	mǎnzú	satisfaction
憤怒	愤怒	fènnù	anger, indignation
瞞		mán	to hide (the truth)
苦心孤詣	苦心孤诣	kǔxīngūyì	painstakingly
即刻		jíkè	立刻
折斷	折断	zhéduàn	to break in half, to snap
翅		chì	wing
擲	掷	zhì	to throw
踏		tà	to trample, to step on
扁		biǎn	flat
論長幼	论长幼	lùnzhǎngyòu	as far as age is concerned
論力氣	论力气	lùnlìqì	as far as strength is concerned
敵	敌	dí	to match
勝利	胜利	shènglì	victory
傲然		àorán	proudly
絕望		juéwàng	in despair
留心		líuxīn	to pay attention to, to think about

懲罰	惩罚	chéngfá	punishment, retribution
輪	轮	lún	to come in turns
偶而		ǒu'ér	by chance
講論	讲论	jiǎnglùn	to discuss
遊戲	游戏	yóuxì	game
正當	正当	zhèngdāng	proper
行爲	行为	xíngwéi	behavior
玩具		wánjù	toy
天使		tiānshǐ	angel
毫不憶及	毫不忆及	háobú yìjí	從來都沒想過
虐殺	虐杀	nüè shā	to eliminate cruelly
展開	展开	zhǎnkāi	to unfold
仿佛		fǎngfú	as if
鉛塊	铅块	qiānkuài	block of lead
墮	堕	duò	to fall, to sink
竟		jìng	actually, all the way
斷絕	断绝	duànjué	to break

補過	补过	bǔguò	to make amends
贊成	赞成	zànchéng	to agree, to approve of
其時	其时	qíshí	at that time
鬍子	胡子	húzi	beard
討	讨	tǎo	to seek
寬恕	宽恕	kuānshù	to forgive
可行的		kěxíngde	feasible
添		tiān	to add
刻		kè	to carve
辛苦		xīnkǔ	hardship, suffering
條紋	条纹	tiáowén	wrinkles
沉重		chénzhòng	heavy
叙述		xùshù	to narrate
寬鬆	宽松	kuānsōng	relieved
全然		quánrán	completely
忘却		wàngquè	to forget
怨恨		yuànhèn	grudge

怨		yuàn	complaint; hatred
謊	谎	huǎng	a lie
希求		xīqiú	to desire; to hope for
異地	异地	yìdì	a strange land
回憶	回忆	huíyì	recollection
一併	一并	yíbìng	together
無可把握	无可把握	wúkěbǎwò	intangible; unable to control
寒威		hánwēi	frigid coldness

风　筝
词语例句

一、在（pronoun; noun）　　　　　　　　　　　　　　　对…来说

　　※　北平的冬季，地上还有积雪，灰黑色的秃树枝桠叉于晴朗的天
　　　　空中，而远处有一、二风筝浮动，在我是一种惊异和悲哀。

　　1．他们多年不和，以至离婚，这在双方都是一种解脱。

　　2．家里有汽车，在美国人是非常普通的事。

二、倘…便…　　　　　　　　　　　　　　要是…就…; 如果…就…

　　※　风筝时节，倘听到沙沙的风轮声，仰头便能看见一个淡墨色的蟹
　　　　风筝。

　　1．在纽约，倘住在中国城，便什么中国货都买得到。

　　2．在这儿，倘能出到十五块钱，便能吃到很像样的晚饭了。

三、显出…模样　　　　　　　　　　　　　to show … appearance

　　※　还有寂寞的瓦片风筝，没有风轮，又放得很低，伶仃地显出憔悴
　　　　可怜模样。

　　1．她听到好消息以后显出兴奋的模样。

　　2．一谈到他的家庭他就显出痛苦的模样。

四、…和…相照应　　　　to match with …; to correspond with …

　　※　地上的杨柳已经发芽，和孩子们天上的点缀相照应，打成一片春
　　　　日的温和。

　　1．天上的白云和起伏的群山相照应，景色格外宜人。

　　2．辉煌的灯火和人们愉快的笑脸相照应，更显出节日的快乐。

五、… Adj.（undesirable）得不堪　　extremely Adj. …; be in
　　　　　　　　　　　　　　　　　　an extremely … situation

※ 他那时大概十岁内外吧，多病，瘦得不堪。

1. 过度的工作使他疲惫不堪。

2. 天下大雨，车又坏在路上，真是狼狈不堪。

3. 这条小街年久失修，房屋都破烂不堪。

六、果然　　　　　　　　　　　　　　as expected

※ 我恍然大悟似的，...推开门，果然就在尘封的什物堆中发现了他。

1. 昨天广播说今天会下雨，今天果然下了大雨。

2. 在中国的经历使他觉得中国果然是历史悠久的国家。

七、论...论...　　　　　　　　as far as ... is concerned

※ 论长幼，论力气，他都是敌不过我的。

1. 论学历，论经验，他都比你强。

2. 论自由，论民主，美国都占领先地位。

八、又有什么...之可言呢?　　What...could there be to speak of?
　　　　　　　　　　　　　　（rhetorical question）

※　全然忘却，毫无怨恨，又有什么宽恕之可言呢?

1. 没有共同语言，又有什么爱情之可言呢?

2. 这么点小事，又有什么感激之可言呢?

九、罢了（used to end a sentence）　　it's only ...; that's all

※ 无怨的恕，说谎罢了。

1. 他只是做了应该做的事罢了。

2. 我没什么成就，只是写了两本书罢了。

（五）

第二的母親

孤兒	孤儿	gū'ér	orphan
認清	认清	rènqīng	to see clearly
面貌		miànmào	face
叔父		shūfù	uncle
嬸母	婶母	shěnmǔ	aunt (wife of father's younger brother)
小厮		xiǎosī	minor male servant
老媽子	老妈子	lǎomāzi	old maid; female servant
照料		zhàoliào	to take care of
僕人	仆人	púrén	servant
寬大	宽大	kuāndà	spacious
伴侶		bànlǚ	companion
究竟		jiūjìng	after all
寂寞		jìmò	lonely
温和		wēnhé	kind; gentle
戲	戏	xì	Beijing Opera; drama

戲園	戏园	xìyuán	theater
少爺	少爷	shàoye	young master
做鬼臉	做鬼脸	zuò guǐliǎn	to make a face
親切	亲切	qīnqiè	loving; kind
撫養	抚养	fǔyǎng	to raise, to nurture
溫暖		wēnnuǎn	warmth
似乎		sìhū	to seem; as if
貧窮	贫穷	pínqióng	poor
寡婦	寡妇	guǎfù	widow
面孔		miànkǒng	face
照例		zhàolì	as usual; usually
僻靜		pìjìng	secluded and quiet
撫着	抚着	fǔzhe	to caress
抱着		bàozhe	to hold in one's arms
快樂	快乐	kuàilè	joy, happiness
得意		déyì	proud
起初		qǐchū	at first

羨慕		xiànmù	to envy
誇耀		kuāyào	to brag about
愛撫	爱抚	aìfǔ	to lovingly caress
可悲		kěbēi	sad, tragic
誇示		kuāshì	to show off
縫	缝	féng	to sew
驕傲	骄傲	jiāo'ào	arrogant; proud
妒忌		dùjì	to be jealous of; to envy
空虛		kōngxū	nothing; void
製造	制造	zhìzào	to create; to make
出乎意料之外		chū hū yìliào zhī wài	beyond expectation
果然		guǒrán	as expected
幼年		yòunián	childhood
單調	单调	dāndiào	dull, monotonous
添		tiān	to add
趣味		qùwèi	delight; interest
點綴	点缀	diǎnzhuì	enhancement

快活		kuàihuo	happy
包厢		bāoxiāng	theater box
台上		táishàng	on the stage
演		yǎn	to perform
武戲	武戏	wǔxì	fighting scene in Chinese opera
光着		guāngzhe	to be stripped
身子		shēnzi	body above waist
翻筋斗		fān jīndou	to turn a somersault
伏		fú	to bend over
欄杆	栏杆	lán'gān	banister; railing
柔軟	柔软	róuruǎn	soft
驚訝	惊讶	jīngyà	astonished
掉過頭	掉过头	diàoguòtóu	to turn around
微笑		wēixiào	to smile
呆呆地		dāidāide	blankly
望		wàng	to stare at
瓜子臉		guāziliǎn	oval face

細	细	xì	thin; fine
眉毛		méimao	eyebrow
粉紅色	粉红色	fěnhóngsè	pink
頰	颊	jiá	cheek
現出	现出	xiànchū	to exhibit
呆相		dāixiàng	a dull look
酒窩	酒窝	jiǔwō	dimple
拉		lā	to pull to draw towards oneself
衣角		yījiǎo	corner of clothing
埋		mái	to bend over
撫摸	抚摸	fǔmō	to stroke, to caress
膝		xī	knee
不時	不时	bùshí	from time to time
詳細	详细	xiángxì	carefully; in detail
解説	解说	jiěshuō	to explain
情節	情节	qíngjié	plot
興味	兴味	xìngwèi	interest

俯下		fǔxià	to bow (one's head)
抬頭	抬头	táitóu	to raise one's head
居然		jūrán	surprisingly
接連	接连	jiēlián	in succession
時時	时时	shíshí	often
渴望		kěwàng	to long for
體貼	体贴	tǐtiē	to show love and concern
緣故	缘故	yuángù	reason
蠢		chǔn	foolish
拍		pāi	to pat
稱呼	称呼	chēnghū	form of address, title of a person
當着...面	当着...面	dāngzhe... miàn	in front of (someone)...
害羞		hàixiū	shy
微微		wēiwēi	slightly
答應	答应	dāyìng	to answer
偷偷地看		tōutōude kàn	to steal a glance at
喜色		xǐsè	joy

下頷 hé

牽	牵	qiān	to lead by holding the hand
轎子	轿子	jiàozi	sedan chair
瞥見		piējiàn	to catch a glimpse of, to catch sight of
睬		cǎi	to pay attention to
絮絮		xùxù	loquatious
甜蜜		tiánmì	sweet
仿佛		fǎngfú	almost as if
懷裏	怀里	huáilǐ	in one's embrace, in one's arms
待		dài	to treat
打發	打发	dǎfā	to send away
引進	引进	yǐnjìn	to lead into
臥室		wòshì	bedroom
天色		tiānsè	color of the sky
明亮		míngliàng	bright
陳設	陈设	chénshè	furnishings, display
家具		jiājù	furniture
佈置	布置	bùzhì	to decorate

清潔	清洁	qīngjié	clean
整齊	整齐	zhěngqí	tidy
藤椅		téngyǐ	cane chair
瓷罎子	瓷坛子	cítánzi	porcelain jar
抓出		zhuāchū	to grab a handful out
糖果		tángguǒ	candy
盛		chéng	to place into (a container)
碟子		diézi	saucer
陪		péi	to accompany
丫頭	丫头	yātou	servant girl, slave girl
壺	壶	hú	kettle
不耐煩	不耐烦	búnàifán	impatient
牆壁	墙壁	qiángbì	wall
一管笛		yīguǎndí	a flute
琵琶		pípá	plucked string instrument
斜掛		xiéguà	to hang on an angle
尊		zūn	measure word for an idol or image

白瓷		báicí	white porcelain
觀音	观音	Guānyīn	Guanyin (a Bodhisattva); the Goddess of Mercy
驚奇	惊奇	jīngqí	to be surprised
立在		lìzài	to stand at
花瓶		huāpíng	vase
風景畫	风景画	fēngjǐnghuà	landscape painting
如今		rújīn	now
忍耐		rěnnài	to bear; to tolerate
搽粉		cháfěn	to powder one's face, to apply makeup
膽怯	胆怯	dǎnqiè	timid
禁不住		jīnbuzhù	to be unable to refrain from
梳頭	梳头	shūtóu	to comb hair
仔細	仔细	zǐxì	meticulously
分開	分开	fēnkāi	to divide
光光的		guāngguāngde	smooth and shiny
緊緊	紧紧	jǐnjǐn	close
靠着		kàozhe	leaning on; touching

感動	感动	gǎndòng	to be touched emotionally, to be moved
不曉得	不晓得	bùxiǎode	不知道
眼角		yǎnjiǎo	the corner of the eye
嵌着		qiànzhe	to be embedded; to inlay
淚珠	泪珠	lèizhū	tear drop
揩		kāi	to wipe
捧		pěng	to hold in both hands
親	亲	qīn	to kiss
染紅	染红	rǎnhóng	to dye red
胭脂		yānzhī	rouge
痕迹		hénjī	mark
濕	湿	shī	wet
陰暗	阴暗	yīn'àn	dark and gloomy
突然		tūrán	suddenly
短襖	短袄	duǎn'ǎo	short Chinese-style jacket
配合		pèihé	to match
吹笛子		chuīdízi	to play the flute

凳子		dèngzi	stool
跪		guì	to kneel
調子	调子	diàozi	melody
面容		miànróng	complexion
竟然		jìngrán	unexpectedly
偎		wēi	to snuggle up to; to lean close to
嘆口氣	叹口气	tànkǒuqì	to sigh
橫在		héngzài	to lay across
直率		zhíshuài	frank, candid
彈琵琶	弹琵琶	tánpípa	to play pipa (a Chinese musical instrument)
相像		xiāngxiàng	to look alike
誠實	诚实	chéngshí	honest
悲苦		bēikǔ	sorrowful
提		tí	to mention
歇		xiē	to rest
半晌		bànshǎng	a while
思索		sīsuǒ	to ponder

公館	公馆	gōngguǎn	a residence of a rich person; a mansion
平静		píngjìng	peaceful
貴重	贵重	guìzhòng	valuable
一口咬定		yì kǒu yǎo dìng	to arbitrarily accuse
硬		yìng	obstinately
冤枉		yuānwǎng	to wrongfully assign blame
開除	开除	kāichú	to expel
當	当	dàng	to pawn
疲倦		píjuàn	tired, weary
呻吟		shēnyín	to groan
守		shǒu	to keep watch over; to look after
饅頭	馒头	mántou	steamed bun
捉住		zhuōzhù	to catch
醫治	医治	yīzhì	to give medical treatment
戲班子	戏班子	xìbānzi	theatrical troupe
治病		zhìbìng	to cure an illness
情願	情愿	qíngyuàn	to be willing to

女角		nǚjué	female role
挨鞭子		áibiānzi	to suffer a whipping
腳步	脚步	jiǎobù	steps, walk
一舉一動	一举一动	yì jǔ yí dòng	every move and action
登台		dēngtái	to take the stage and perform
漸漸	渐渐	jiànjiàn	gradually
名角		míngjué	famous actor or actress
大人老爺	大人老爷	dàrén lǎoyé	people of importance, rich VIPs
包圍	包围	bāowéi	to surround
掙錢	挣钱	zhèngqián	to make money
敷衍		fūyǎn	to unwillingly do sth. to please others
出賣	出卖	chūmài	to sell
皮肉		píròu	flesh
妓女		jìnǚ	prostitute
欠債	欠债	qiànzhài	to be in debt
捧場	捧场	pěngchǎng	to attend to show support
眼睜睜		yǎn zhēngzhēng	(looking on) helplessly

45

戲子	戏子	xìzi	actor or actress
贖	赎	shú	to redeem
滿心		mǎnxīn	to...with all one's heart
脫離	脱离	tuōlí	to escape from, to remove oneself from
苦海		kǔhǎi	the abyss of misery
悲聲	悲声	bēishēng	sad voice
嘆息	叹息	tànxī	to sigh
茫然		mángrán	blankly
疑心		yíxīn	to doubt
惶惑		huánghuò	startled and perplexed
否定		fǒudìng	to deny
配		pèi	to qualify
福氣	福气	fúqì	luck
志向		zhìxiàng	ambition
姨太太		yítàitai	concubine
過活	过活	guòhuó	過日子
分辨		fēnbiàn	to differentiate

尋常	寻常	xúncháng	usual, ordinary
壓倒	压倒	yādǎo	to overwhelm
手帕		shǒupà	handkerchief
默默地		mòmòde	silently
分別		fēnbié	to separate
相片		xiàngpiān	photograph
求		qiú	to implore, to beg
橢圓形	椭圆形	tuǒyuánxíng	oval
金墜子	金坠子	jīnzhuìzi	pendant
金鏈子	金链子	jīnliànzi	gold chain
垂		chuí	to hang down
胸前		xiōngqián	bosom
蓋子	盖子	gàizi	cover, lid
可憐	可怜	kělián	poor, pitiful
照片		zhàopiān	photograph
紀念	纪念	jìniàn	souvenir, momento
抖		dǒu	to shake, to shiver

安慰		ānwèi	to comfort
唤		huàn	叫
覺醒	觉醒	juéxǐng	to awaken
推開	推开	tuīkāi	to push away
咳嗽		késòu	cough
答覆	答复	dáfù	to answer, to reply
淚痕	泪痕	lèihén	tear marks
抱歉		bàoqiàn	to apologize
道		dào	measure word for a dish in a meal
主人		zhǔrén	host
上年紀	上年纪	shàngniánjì	to be getting on in years
解釋	解释	jiěshì	to explain
不禁		bùjīn	to be unable to refrain from
失笑		shīxiào	to laugh
擺	摆	bǎi	to set (a table)
周到		zhōudào	considerate, thoughtful
表現出	表现出	biǎoxiànchū	to show; to exhibit

不捨	不舍	bùshě	to be unwilling to part; to be reluctant to part
鼓勵	鼓励	gǔlì	encouragement
襲來	袭来	xílái	to come (surprisingly)
災禍	灾祸	zāihuò	disaster
奪走	夺走	duózǒu	to snatch away
料理		liàolǐ	to take care of, to attend to
喪事	丧事	sāngshì	funeral arrangements
處理	处理	chǔlǐ	to deal with, to handle
遺產	遗产	yíchǎn	property left by the deceased
監護	监护	jiānhù	to guard
即使		jíshǐ	even if; even though
反抗		fǎnkàng	to resist
羈絆	羁绊	jībàn	fetters; shackles
解放		jiěfàng	to liberate
強壯	强壮	qiángzhuàng	strong and sturdy
尋找	寻找	xúnzhǎo	to look for, to seek
回報	回报	huíbào	to repay

寬廣	宽广	kuān'guǎng	broad
開設	开设	kāishè	to set up
興隆	兴隆	xīnglóng	prosperous
洋貨店	洋货店	yánghuòdiàn	store selling foreign goods
玩偶		wán'ǒu	play thing; doll
脆弱		cuìruò	weak and fragile
消滅	消灭	xiāomiè	to perish, to cease to exist
憐惜	怜惜	liánxī	pity
悲痛		bēitòng	anguish, sorrow
合理		hélǐ	reasonable
折磨		zhémó	to torture
悲慘	悲惨	bēicǎn	miserable
命運	命运	mìngyùn	fate
憤怒	愤怒	fènnù	indignance
詛咒	诅咒	zǔzhòu	curse, imprecation

第二的母亲

词语例句

一、把…当作…   to take … as …

※ 叔父没有小孩，就把我当作他的儿子。

1. 把东亚研究当作专业的人越来越多。

2. 她把老师当作自己的好朋友。

二、究竟   毕竟，after all

※ 小厮和老妈子的世界跟我这个孩子的世界究竟不同。

1. 我们究竟是老朋友，不会计较这点小事。

2. 你怎么还干涉他的私事，他究竟不是小孩子了。

三、究竟   到底

※ 他一天究竟做些什么事情呢?

1. 你究竟爱不爱他?

2. 这些东西究竟是从哪儿弄来的?

四、似乎   好像

※ 他知道的事情比我多，但是他似乎并不聪明。

1. 中国似乎并没有我想像的那么落后。

2. 我发现他似乎很有音乐天才。

五、以…作（为）中心   to take … as the centre

※ 他的故事总是以母亲作中心。

1. 这是一部以爱情作中心的影片。

2. 他以收集古董作为生活的中心。

六、不管…   no matter …

※ 不管怎样，和母亲见面就是这个儿子最大的快乐。

1. 不管环境多么艰苦，他都能保持乐观。

2. 不管别人说什么，我都要坚持走自己的路。

七、不时　　　　　　　　　　　　　　　　from time to time

※ 他不时抚摸我的头发。

1. 大自然不时给人类带来灾难。

2. 六十岁以后，他的心脏病不时发作。

八、居然　　　　　　　　　　　　　　　　surprisingly

※ …我居然接连叫了两声"妈妈!"

1. 他没上过大学，居然当了教授。

2. 他的女朋友生在美国，居然说一口道地的汉语。

九、仿佛　　　　　　　　　　　　　　　　好像

※ 我仿佛觉得就是坐在母亲的怀里了。

1. 跟孩子们在一块儿，我仿佛回到了童年时代。

2. 从中国回来后他仿佛变了一个人。

十、明明　　　　　　　　　　　　obviously; without a doubt

※ 看见这尊观音，我很惊奇，这明明是我们家里的东西。

1. 这明明是你的错，你为什么不承认?

2. 这明明只是经济问题，他偏说是政治问题。

十一、禁不住　　　　　　　　　to be unable to refrain from

※ 我望着这张美丽的面孔，禁不住在心里想: 我果然有一个这样好看
的婶母吗?

1. 想到就要和亲人相见，他禁不住加快了脚步。

2. 听到他受的苦，我禁不住泪流满面。

十二、竟然　　　　　　　　　　　　　（＝居然），unexpectedly

※ 我听着笛声，不知道怎样，竟然想哭了。

1. 真没想到，呆头呆脑的他竟然成了大明星。

2. 那本畅销书的作者竟然是个中学生。

十三、硬 V.　　　　　　　　　　　　　　　　obstinately

※ 别人硬冤枉他，说他把东西偷走了。

1. 他要当歌星，父母却硬要他学科学。

2. 他硬要去就让他去吧。

十四、和...没有两样　　　　　　　　　　exactly the same as

※ 他为了要挣钱，不得不去敷衍别人，陪人睡觉，和妓女简直没有
两样。

1. 这个外国人和本地人简直没有两样。

2. 这样不择手段赚钱简直和抢劫没有两样。

十五、给...捧场　　　　　　　　to attend to show support to ...

※ 大人老爷们也不大高兴来给他捧场了。

1. 你演讲我一定来给你捧场。

2. 他初次登台，朋友们都来给他捧场。

十六、眼睁睁...　　　　　　　　　（looking on) helplessly

※ 他眼睁睁看着就要去走许多老戏子走过的路。

1. 你怎么可以眼睁睁让小偷跑了?

2. 地震发生时，人只能眼睁睁看着它破坏一切。

（六）

奴 隸 的 心

奴隸	奴隶	núlì	slave; servant
祖先		zǔxiān	ancestors
彭		Péng	(surname)
驕傲	骄傲	jiāoào	proud; arrogant
得意		déyì	to be proud of oneself
數目	数目	shùmù	amount
惋惜		wǎnxī	to feel sorry
黃金時代	黄金时代	huángjīnshídài	golden age
舉動	举动	jǔdòng	act
記憶	记忆	jìyì	memory
曾祖		zēngzǔ	great-grand father
志願		zhìyuàn	wish; aspiration
慚愧	惭愧	cánkuì	to be ashamed
發狂	发狂	fākuáng	to go crazy
來歷	来历	láilì	background; origin

結識	结识	jiēshí	to become acquainted with
偶然		ǒurán	by chance; accidentally
闖進	闯进	chuǎngjìn	to run into
駛	驶	shǐ	to drive
車夫	车夫	chēfū	driver
按		àn	to push down
喇叭		lǎbā	car horn
挨		āi	to touch
鐵腕	铁腕	tiěwàn	iron hand (wrist)
拖		tuō	to pull
跌倒		diēdǎo	to fall
安然		ānrán	safely
定神		dìngshén	to pull oneself together
瘦長		shòucháng	thin and tall
板着面孔		bǎnzhemiànkǒng	to keep a straight face
鋒利	锋利	fēnglì	sharp
昂然		ángrán	proudly

交換		jiāohuàn	to exchange
一瞥		yìpiē	a quick glance
冷淡		lěngdàn	cheerless; cold
客套話	客套话	kètàohuà	polite formula; greetings
一針見血	一针见血	yìzhēnjiànxiě	sharply; pierce to the truth with a single pertinent remark
好奇		hàoqí	curiosity
溫情		wēnqíng	tenderheartedness; lenient
無論	无论	wúlùn	no matter
顯得	显得	xiǎndé	to appear
冷酷		lěngkù	cruel
身世		shēnshì	life experience
節儉	节俭	jiéjiǎn	frugal
習氣	习气	xíqì	bad habit
染到		rǎndào	to acquire (a bad habit)
西裝		xīzhuāng	suit (Western style outfit)
寢室	寝室	qǐnshì	dorm room
操場	操场	cāochǎng	playground

顧	顾	gù	to care; to take into account
沉默		chénmò	reticent
思索		sīsuǒ	to ponder
忍不住		rěnbuzhù	can not help (doing)
掉頭	掉头	diàotóu	to turn away
陰沉	阴沉	yīnchén	sombre; gloomy
孤僻		gūpì	unsociable and eccentric
留心		liúxīn	to pay more attention
結交	结交	jiéjiāo	to make (friends)
便是		biànshì	even if
露出		lùchū	to reveal; to show
雜	杂	zá	sundry; various
古怪		gǔguài	eccentric; strange
著者		zhùzhě	author
除非		chúfēi	unless
從頭至尾	从头至尾	cóngtóuzhìwěi	from beginning to end
新闢的	新辟的	xīnpìde	newly established

高爾夫	高尔夫	gāoěrfū	golf
拂		fú	to flick; to wipe off
夾袍		jiápáo	lined gown
灰塵	灰尘	huīchén	dust
半晌		bànshǎng	quite a while
埋下頭	埋下头	máixiàtóu	to bury one's head
攤開	摊开	tānkāi	to spread open
鄭	郑	Zhèng	(surname)
低沉		dīchén	low and deep
是否		shìfǒu	是不是
素來		sùlái	always
何止		hézhǐ	far more than
苦惱	苦恼	kǔnǎo	vexed
意義	意义	yìyì	significance
擴大	扩大	kuòdà	to expand; to broaden
無論如何	无论如何	wúlùnrúhé	anyway; anyhow; in any case
總	总	zǒng	after all

慶幸	庆幸	qìngxìng	rejoicingly
藐視	藐视	miǎoshì	to look down upon
射		shè	to shoot (eyesight); to look sharply
含		hán	to include
輕蔑	轻蔑	qīngmiè	disdain
羨慕		xiànmù	admiration
妒嫉		dùjí	jealousy
作怪		zuòguài	to do mischief
憐憫	怜悯	liánmǐn	pity
出乎意料之外		chūhū yìliào zhīwài	unexpectedly
叙說	叙说	xùshuō	to narrate
功績	功绩	gōngjī	achievements
驚疑	惊疑	jīngyí	surprised and bewildered
謙虛	谦虚	qiānxū	modest
驚奇	惊奇	jīngqí	surprised
神氣	神气	shénqì	facial expression; air
後人	后人	hòurén	descendants

傲慢		àomàn	arrogant
捧		pěng	to hold in both hands
侮辱		wǔrǔ	to humiliate
氣憤	气愤	qìfèn	indignantly
高祖		gāozǔ	great-great-grandfather
商人		shāngrén	trader; merchant
後裔	后裔	hòuyì	offspring
華麗	华丽	huálì	gorgeous
府第		fǔdì	mansion
姬妾		jīqiè	concubine
報復	报复	bàofù	to retaliate; to revenge
憎怒		zēngnù	hateful
恢復	恢复	huīfù	to return to
心境		xīnjìng	state of mind
恩		ēn	favor
自豪		zìháo	proud
若干		ruògān	a certain amount

譏刺	讥刺	jīcì	satire
被窩	被窝	bèiwō	a quilt folded to form a sleeping bag
恨不得		hènbudé	one would if one could
諱言	讳言	huìyán	would not speak up
宣布		xuānbù	to declare
設法	设法	shèfǎ	想辦法
免得		miǎndé	so as to avoid
意外		yìwài	unexpected
忠心		zhōngxīn	loyal; devoted
辛辛苦苦		xīnxīnkǔkǔ	to take great pains
公館	公馆	gōngguǎn	residence of rich people
服侍		fúshì	to serve
責罵	责骂	zémà	to dress down; to yell at
應	应	yìng	to respond; to answer
搖撼		yáohàn	to shake to the foundation
縫隙	缝隙	fèngxì	crack; crevice
壯年	壮年	zhuàngnián	the more robust years of a person's life

枯枝敗葉	枯枝败叶	kūzhībàiyè	withered twigs and dead leaves
烤火		kǎohuǒ	to warm by a fire
話匣子	话匣子	huàxiázi	chatterbox; mouth
正直		zhèngzhí	fair-minded
誠實	诚实	chéngshí	honest
好報	好报	hǎobào	reward; good requitement
番		fān	measure word for words
吊死		diàosǐ	to hang by the neck
槐樹	槐树	huáishù	Chinese scholar tree
尸首		shīshǒu	corpse
席子		xízi	mat
污穢	污秽	wūhuì	filthy
分辯	分辩	fēnbiàn	to defend oneself (against a charge)
一記耳光	一记耳光	yìjì ěrguāng	a slap in the face
賠償	赔偿	péicháng	to compensate (for a loss)
信任		xìnrèn	trust
報答	报答	bàodá	to repay

恩典		ēndiǎn	favour; grace
積蓄	积蓄	jīxù	savings
竊賊	窃贼	qièzéi	thief
孫子	孙子	sūnzi	grandson
懷裏	怀里	huáilǐ	in one's arms
慈祥		cíxiáng	kindly
淌眼淚	淌眼泪	tǎng yǎnlèi	to shed tears
迷		mí	to blur
分辨		fēnbiàn	to distinguish
屬牛	属牛	shǔniú	born in the year of the ox
揩		kāi	擦
安慰		ānwèi	to comfort
爲難	为难	wéinán	to feel awkward
遲疑	迟疑	chíyí	to hesitate
嘆氣	叹气	tànqì	to sigh
賭咒		dǔzhòu	to take an oath
發誓	发誓	fāshì	to swear

斷送	断送	duànsòng	to ruin; to forfeit
略略		luèluè	briefly
編造	编造	biānzào	to make up
默默地		mòmòde	silently
愁容		chóuróng	worried look
連忙	连忙	liánmáng	to hasten to
躲		duǒ	to hide
頸項	颈项	jǐngxiàng	neck
溫和		wēnhé	tenderly; mildly
爹爹		diēdie	daddy
寂然		jìrán	quiet and still
喚		huàn	to call out
許久	许久	xǔjiǔ	很久
淚痕	泪痕	lèihén	tear stains
聽從	听从	tīngcóng	to obey
與其A不如B	与其A不如B	yǔqí...bùrú...	it's better B than A
血統	血统	xuètǒng	blood lineage

延長	延长	yáncháng	to extend
出頭	出头	chūtóu	to free from (misery)
固然		gùrán	it is true that
修飾	修饰	xiūshì	to modify
多少		duōshǎo	more or less
喃喃		nánnán	to mutter
捨得	舍得	shěde	to give up
袖子		xiùzi	sleeve
垂		chuí	to let fall
監牢	监牢	jiānláo	prison
違背	违背	wéibèi	to run counter to; to break (a promise)
諾言	诺言	nuòyán	promise
仇人		chóurén	personal enemy
犧牲	牺牲	xīshēng	to sacrifice
痙攣	痉挛	jìngluán	convulsion; spasm
極力	极力	jílì	to do one's utmost
嘴唇皮		zuǐchúnpí	lip

爆發	爆发	bàofā	eruption
隱匿	隐匿	yǐnnì	to hide
探索		tànsuǒ	exploring
放鬆	放松	fàngsōng	to relax; to loosen
隱衷	隐衷	yǐnzhōng	feelings one wishes to keep to oneself
羞愧		xiūkuì	shame
隱藏	隐藏	yǐncáng	to hide
陪		péi	to accompany
仿佛		fǎng fú	好像
開恩	开恩	kāi' ēn	to bestow favour
發慈悲	发慈悲	fācíbēi	to show mercy
床沿		chuángyán	the edge of a bed
奔		bèn	to go straight towards
學堂	学堂	xuétáng	(old term for) school
斜		xié	to recline
俯		fǔ	to bow (one's head)
嗚嗚	呜呜	wūwū	(onomatopoeia) sound of weeping

體貼	体贴	tǐtiē	to give every care to
鼓舞		gǔwǔ	to encourage
謝罪	谢罪	xièzuì	to apologize for an offense
饒恕	饶恕	ráoshù	to forgive
仍舊	仍旧	réngjiù	還是
情願		qíngyuàn	would rather
前世		qiánshì	previous existence
冤孽		yuānniè	wrong and sin
伺候		cìhòu	to serve; to wait upon
胡纏	胡缠	húchán	to harass with unreasonable demands
拿...開心	拿...开心	ná...kāixīn	to enjoy oneself at other's expense
端正		duānzhèng	good-looking
顧惜	顾惜	gùxī	to show care and pity
罷了	罢了	bàle	(used at end of sentence) it's only...
蒙住		méngzhù	to cover
依舊	依旧	yījiù	as before; still
盡量	尽量	jìnliàng	to the best of one's ability

吞食		tūnshí	to engulf
彼岸		bǐ àn	the other shore
鬼魂		guǐhún	ghost; spirit
境地		jìngdì	plight
忍耐		rěnnài	to restrain oneself; to tolerate
費工夫	费工夫	fèigōngfu	to take time
光景		guāngjǐng	time
討 (老婆)	讨 (老婆)	tǎo (laǒpó)	to marry (a woman)
卑賤	卑贱	bēijiàn	lowly
生存		shēngcún	life; existence
被誣爲	被诬为	bèiwūwéi	to be accused falsely of
代人受罪		dàirénshòuzuì	to suffer for the crime of another
獄	狱	yù	jail
姦污	奸污	jiānwū	to rape
污點	污点	wūdiǎn	blemish; smirch
嘲笑		cháoxiào	to ridicule; to laugh at
鄙視	鄙视	bǐshì	to look down upon

折磨		zhémó	to suffer; to torment
悲泣		bēiqì	to weep with grief
沉醉		chénzuì	to become intoxicated
受刑		shòuxíng	to be put to torture
任...V.		rèn...V....	to do...at one's discretion
調笑	调笑	tiáoxiào	to poke fun at; to assail with obscenities
惡毒	恶毒	èdú	vicious
詛咒	诅咒	zǔzhòu	curse; imprecation
抵抗		dǐkàng	to resist; to stand up to
景物		jǐngwù	scenery
燃		rán	to light; to burn
輝煌	辉煌	huīhuáng	brilliantly illuminated
侍僕	侍仆	shìpú	servant
徘徊		páihuái	to pace up and down
半裸		bànluǒ	half naked
打扮		dǎbàn	to dress up
安閑	安闲	ānxián	leisurely

朝		cháo	towards
良心		liángxīn	conscience
無窮	无穷	wúqióng	endless
蕩漾	荡漾	dàngyàng	to rise and fall, ripple, undulate
無情	无情	wúqíng	ruthless, merciless, heartless
幅		fú	measure word for paintings and pictures
晃來晃去		huàngláihuàngqù	to sway and shake back and forth
陷害		xiànhài	to frame; to make false charge against
恐怖		kǒngbù	terrible
攫取		juéqǔ	to grab; to seize
捕獲物	捕获物	bǔhuòwù	things captured; bag
轉	转	zhuàn	to rotate; to revolve
末日		mò'rì	doomsday; Day of Judgment; end
驚恐	惊恐	jīngkǒng	terrified; panic-stricken
鎮静	镇静	zhènjìng	calm; unruffled; composed; cool
凶惡	凶恶	xiōngè	fierce; ferocious; fiendish
當初	当初	dāngchū	in the first place; at that time

70

輾死	辗死	niǎnsǐ	to flatten to death; to be crushed to death
不作聲	不作声	búzuòshēng	to be quiet
謀	谋	móu	to seek; to work for
甘願		gānyuàn	willingly; readily
悔恨		huǐhèn	to regret deeply; to repent bitterly
所謂	所谓	suǒwèi	the so-called
傳給	传给	chuángěi	to pass on; to hand down
胸膛		xiōngtáng	chest
鮮紅	鲜红	xiānhóng	scarlet; bright red
法蘭絨	法兰绒	fǎlánróng	flannel
遮住		zhēzhù	to cover; to hide
竟		jìng	actually
全然		quánrán	entirely
悲哀		bēi'āi	grieved; sorrowful
昏亂	昏乱	hūnluàn	dazed and confused; befuddled
脚迹		jiǎojī	footprint; track
疏遠	疏远	shūyuǎn	to become estranged

娛樂	娱乐	yúlè	amusement; entertainment; recreation
果然		guǒrán	just as expected
納涼	纳凉	nàliáng	to enjoy the cool (in the open air)
翻閱	翻阅	fānyuè	to leaf through; to glance over
本埠		běnbù	this port; wharf
欄	栏	lán	column
則	则	zé	measure word for a piece of writing
槍斃	枪毙	qiāngbì	to execute by shooting
記事	记事	jìshì	record of events
忘卻		wàngquè	忘記
浮現	浮现	fúxiàn	to appear before one's eyes
歉然		qiànrán	apologetic; regretful
伸		shēn	to stretch out; to extend
撫摩	抚摩	fǔmó	to stroke
溫柔		wēnróu	gentle and soft
驚訝	惊讶	jīngyà	astonished; astounded; surprised

奴隶的心
词语例句

一、无论…都…   no matter

※ 无论在什么地方，他都显得是一个冷酷的人。

1. 他无论说什么语言都带有上海口音。

2. 东西方文化无论在哪方面都有差别。

二、越…愈加…   越…越…

※ 我越不懂，便愈加想了解它。

1. 我越了解他，愈加觉得他是个了不起的人。

2. 政府越控制得严，老百姓愈加渴望自由。

三、除非   unless

※ 那些书的内容，我完全不知道，除非我自己拿来从头至尾地读过
   一遍。

1. 若要人不知，除非己莫为。

2. 人与人之间的矛盾是不可避免的，除非不跟人交往。

四、何止   far more than

※ 几百万? 实际上何止几千万?

1. 他对你何止是同情? 你难道没感觉到吗?

2. 申请这个学校的学生何止几十人? 有好几百人呢!

五、对…加以…   对…进行…

※ 对于一个领有十六个奴隶的人，居然加以藐视。

1. 中国的政策是要对社会制度加以改革。

2. 对吸毒的青少年加以教育是社会的责任。

六、...在作怪   to do mischief; to make trouble

※ 我忽然想明白了，我以为大概是妒嫉在作怪吧。

1. 他极力反对不同人种之间的婚姻，是他的保守观念在作怪。

2. 由于种族歧视的思想作怪，他反对雇佣少数民族。

七、出乎意料之外...   contrary to one's expectations

※ 出乎我的意料之外，他又把眼光向我射来，这一次他的眼光里充满了骄傲。

1. 早上还是狂风暴雨，下午却出乎意料之外的天晴了。

2. 出乎大家的意料之外，公司提升了老张做部门主管。

八、明明   obviously

※ 你明明说你的祖先是奴隶。

1. 市场经济明明是资本主义的东西，社会主义的中国怎么会采用呢?

2. 中国明明是第三世界的国家，在国际贸易中不应该以发达国家的标准来对待。

九、以...自豪   to be proud of

※ 我以作奴隶的后人自豪。

1. 他以自己的成就自豪。

2. 他以作一个好教师自豪。

十、恨不得   one would if one could; how one wishes one could

※ 我恨不得使你们这般人的眼睛睁大一点。

1. 他恨不得中文说得跟中国人一样好。

2. 我恨不得让中国一夜之间就成为发达国家。

十一、免得   so as not to; so as to avoid

※ 我想设法骗他出去，免得他在这里有什么意外的举动。

1．你最好向他解释清楚，免得有误会。

2．请你停下车问问路，免得走错了。

3．经济不景气，各家公司都赶紧裁员，免得遭受更大损失。

十二、再没有 V...   never

※ 我再没有看见比他更忠心的人。

1．到了美国以后，他再没有担心政治迫害。

2．我再没有听到比这更可怕的故事。

十四、加以...   再说；而且

※ 他越想越苦恼，加以他做了多年的奴隶，并没有积蓄，赔不起这
  一笔钱。

1．这个社会没有平等，加以缺乏自由，早晚是会发生革命的。

2．这种车漂亮、结实、耐用，加以价格便宜，所以很受顾客欢迎。

十五、V.个不止   to do ... incessantly（without end）

※ 父亲抱着我哭个不止。

1．他们一碰到一起就吵个不止。

2．一提起他的家人他就说个不止。

十六、与其 A 不如 B   doing A is not as good as doing
                           B; It's better B than A

※ 与其活着，...还不如由我把这条命卖给主人，让牛儿读点书，将
  来...

1．与其在家发牢骚，不如出去赚点钱。

2．去纽约与其开车，不如坐火车。

十七、固然   it is true that ..., but ...

※ ...，固然我把他的话修饰了一下，但是你总可以感到那颗心还在这些话里跳动吧。

1．多读书固然有用，但也不能忽视实际经验。

2．你固然没有因种族问题而受到歧视，但这不能说明歧视不存在。

十八、（要）不是...　　　　　　　　　if it's not ...

※ 不是为你，我情愿跟你爹到地下去。

1．要不是改革开放，国民经济怎么会发展得这么快。

2．要不是工作太重，他也不会那么累。

十九、情愿　　　　　　　　　would rather

※ 不是为你，我情愿跟你爹到地下去。

1．他情愿死，也不要不自由。

2．我情愿考不及格，也不愿意作弊。

（七）

手

紫		zǐ	purple
指甲		zhǐjia	fingernail
手腕		shǒuwàn	wrist
怪物		guàiwù	creature, monster
地板		dìbǎn	floor
繞	绕	rào	to move around, to circle
點名	点名	diǎnmíng	to take attendance
忍		rěn	to endure, to bear
忍不住		rěnbuzhù	to be unable to bear
迅速		xùnsù	rapid
有規律地	有规律地	yǒu guīlǜ de	orderly
催促		cuīcù	to urge, to hasten
垂		chuí	to hang down, to let fall
肩頭	肩头	jiāntóu	shoulder
天花板		tiānhuābǎn	ceiling

77

慌亂	慌乱	huāngluàn	to be flustered, to be alarmed and bewildered
仍舊	仍旧	réngjiù	still, yet
莊嚴	庄严	zhuāngyán	solemn, dignified
移動	移动	yídòng	to move, to shift
麻子臉	麻子脸	mázuliǎn	a pockmarked face
顫慄	颤栗	chànlì	to shiver, to tremble
安然		ānrán	peacefully, at ease
饅頭	馒头	mántou	steamed bun
地理		dìlǐ	geography
墨西哥		Mòxīgē	Mexico
白銀	白银	báiyín	silver
雲南	云南	Yúnnán	Yunnan Province
大理石		dàlǐshí	marble
躲		duǒ	to hide (oneself)
將	将	jiāng	to be about to
樓梯	楼梯	lóutī	stairs, staircase
樹枝	树枝	shùzhī	branch, twig

白絨	白绒	báiróng	white flannel
穗頭	穗头	suìtou	tassel, fringe
長筒	长筒	chángtǒng	long and tube-shaped
過道	过道	guòdào	corridor, passageway
盡頭	尽头	jìntóu	end
窗台		chuāngtái	windowsill
拍打		pāidǎ	to tap, to pat, to beat
空洞		kōngdòng	hollow, empty
嗡聲	嗡声	wēngshēng	buzz, hum
安寧	安宁	ānníng	tranquility
攤	摊	tān	to spread out, to lay out
膝頭	膝头	xītóu	knee
喚醒		huànxǐng	to wake up, to awaken
招呼		zhāohu	to call, to greet
生澀	生涩	shēngsè	unfamiliar and awkward
每逢		měiféng	everytime when
鈍重	钝重	dùnzhòng	blunt, bluntly

曲裏拐彎	曲里拐弯	qūlǐguǎiwān	winding
長蟲	长虫	chángchong	snake
靈活	灵活	línghuó	quick-witted
末尾		mòwěi	end
單字	单字	dānzì	vocabulary
媽的	妈的	māde	Damn!
聖人	圣人	shèngrén	sage, wise man
人情		rénqíng	human relationships
手套		shǒutào	gloves
開春	开春	kāichūn	spring arrives
接見室	接见室	jiējiànshì	reception room
嚷		rǎng	to yell, to shout
二姨		èryí	second aunt
串門	串门	chuànmén	to visit or gossip from door to door
豆子		dòuzi	bean
醃	腌	yān	to salt, to pickle
罐子		guànzi	pot, jar

葱		cōng	scallion
流汗		liúhàn	to sweat, to perspire
耽誤工夫	耽误工夫	dānwù gōngfu	to take up precious time
冒氣	冒气	màoqì	to emit vapor, to steam
閱報室	阅报室	yuèbàoshì	newspaper reading room
茶壺	茶壶	cháhú	teapot
校役		xiàoyì	manual worker such as a janitor, cleaner, etc. in a school
賞錢	赏钱	shǎngqián	to tip; tip
學堂	学堂	xuétáng	school (archaic)
肥皂		féizào	soap
燙	烫	tàng	to scald
早操		zǎocāo	morning exercise
操場	操场	cāochǎng	sports field, playground
豎	竖	shù	to erect, to set upright
貧血	贫血	pínxuè	anemia, anemic
化石		huàshí	fossil
透明		tòumíng	transparent

觸動	触动	chùdòng	to touch and move slightly
抑止		yìzhǐ	to restrain
呼吸		hūxī	breath; to breathe
接觸	接触	jiēchù	to touch
褪		tuì	(of color) fade
手心		shǒuxīn	the palm of the hand
皮膚	皮肤	pífū	skin
強		qiáng	good
散步		sànbù	to go for a walk, to go for a stroll
咳嗽		késòu	to cough
消融		xiāoróng	to melt
鈴	铃	líng	bell
楊樹	杨树	yángshù	poplar tree
抽芽		chōuyá	to bud
蒸發	蒸发	zhēngfā	to evaporate
指揮官	指挥官	zhǐhuīguān	commander
口笛		kǒudí	whistle

振鳴	振鸣	zhènmíng	to reverberate
樹叢	树丛	shùcóng	grove, thicket
回應	回应	huíyìng	response
蔭影	荫影	yìnyǐng	shade
乾縮	干缩	gānsuō	withered
邊緣	边缘	biānyuán	edge
蠻野	蛮野	mányě	wild, uncivilized
强壯	强壮	qiángzhuàng	strong
陷下		xiànxià	to sink, to cave in
肺病		fèibìng	tuberculosis
倒拔		dàobá	to pull up
參觀	参观	cān'guān	to visit, to look around
抹		mǒ	to wipe, to wipe away
慘白	惨白	cǎnbái	dreadfully pale
撕		sī	to tear, to rip
領口	领口	lǐngkǒu	collarband, neckband
漆皮		qīpí	black patent leather

晶亮		jīngliàng	shining, glittering
踢		tī	to kick
玩藝	玩艺	wányì	thing (derogatory)
馬車夫	马车夫	mǎchēfū	carriage driver
涼爽		liángshuǎng	pleasantly cool, nice and cool
黃昏		huánghūn	dusk
染		rǎn	to dye
鋪路	铺路	pūlù	to surface a road
零碎		língsuì	odds and ends, bits and pieces
台階	台阶	táijiē	a flight of steps, steps leading up to a house
閃開	闪开	shǎnkāi	to get out of the way, to make way
腰帶	腰带	yāodài	waistband, belt
抖		dǒu	to shake
遮		zhē	to cover, to hide from view
被子		bèizi	quilt
脫落		tuōluò	to fall off
包袱		bāofu	a bundle wrapped in cloth

圍繞	围绕	wéirào	to surround, to encircle
被褥		bèirù	quilt and mattress
下巴		xiàba	chin
舒暢	舒畅	shūchàng	happy, entirely free from worry
鎮壓	镇压	zhènyā	to suppress, to repress
舍監	舍监	shèjiān	dormitory superintendent
光澤	光泽	guāngzé	gloss, luster, sheen
衛生	卫生	wèishēng	hygiene
角落		jiǎoluò	corner
白眼球		báiyǎnqiú	the whites of the eyes
嗅		xiù	to smell
挨		āi	to be next to
滑稽		huájī	funny, amusing
骯髒	肮脏	āngzāng	filthy, dirty
虱子		shīzi	louse
多餘	多余	duōyú	unnecessary
熄燈	熄灯	xīdēng	to put out the light

捲	卷	juǎn	to roll up
好歹		hǎodǎi	good and bad
供給	供给	gōngjǐ	to provide
學費	学费	xuéfèi	tuition
舌頭	舌头	shétou	tongue
轉彎	转弯	zhuǎnwān	to bend, to turn
厭煩	厌烦	yànfán	to be fed up with, to be sick of
顏料	颜料	yánliào	pigment, dye
襪子	袜子	wàzi	socks, stockings
礬	矾	fán	alum
鷄子	鸡子	jīzǐ	chicken egg
端		duān	to carry, to hold level with both hands
咆哮		páoxiāo	to roar, to thunder
光郎		guānglang	(onomatopoeia)
抛		pāo	to throw, to toss
占據	占据	zhànjù	to occupy
衝	冲	chōng	to rush, to charge

撲	扑	pū	to throw oneself on, to pounce on
照例		zhàolì	as usual
凍木	冻木	dòngmù	to be frozen stiff, numb with cold
咒詛	咒诅	zhòuzǔ	to curse
怨恨		yuànhèn	to have a grudge against somebody
混蛋		húndàn	Bastard!
模糊不清		móhúbùqīng	vague, unclear
遮蔽		zhēbì	to cover, to hide
石階	石阶	shíjiē	stone steps
心臟	心脏	xīnzàng	heart
半夜三更		bànyè sān jīng	late at night, in the middle of the night
及格		jígé	to pass a test, examination, etc.
地下室		dìxiàshì	basement, cellar
蒼黃	苍黄	cānghuáng	yellow and pale
顫索	颤索	chànsuǒ	to shiver, to tremble
屠場	屠场	túchǎng	an abattoir (slaughter house)
馬利亞	马利亚	Mǎlìyà	transliteration of Maria

昏倒		hūndǎo	to pass out, to swoon
沉悶	沉闷	chénmèn	depressing, oppressive
空朗朗		kōnglǎnglǎng	empty, deserted
寂静		jìjìng	quiet, silent
摸索		mōsuǒ	to grope, to feel about
掩住		yǎnzhù	to cover, to conceal
抖		dǒu	to shiver, to tremble
逃開	逃开	táokāi	to escape, to run away
横		héng	to place horizontally
滚落		gǔnluò	to roll down
染缸房		rǎn'gāngfáng	dyeing mill
敲		qiāo	to knock
定親	定亲	dìngqīn	to get engaged
婆婆		pópo	mother-in-law
匹		pǐ	measure word for cloth
居多		jūduō	to be in the majority
牆根	墙根	qiánggēn	the foot of a wall

告別		gàobié	to bid farewell, to say good-bye
出發	出发	chūfā	to set out, to start off
栅欄	栅栏	zhàlán	railings, bars
呼喘		hūchuǎn	to gasp for breath, to be out of breath
隨手	随手	suíshǒu	conveniently, without extra trouble
費力	费力	fèilì	to use great effort
模仿		mófǎng	to imitate
地圖	地图	dìtú	map
痕迹		hénjī	mark, trace
顫抖	颤抖	chàndǒu	to shake, to shiver
雀		què	sparrow
巢		cháo	nest
氈靴	毡靴	zhānxuē	felt boots
脖子		bózi	neck
鬍鬚	胡须	húxū	beard, moustache or whiskers
冰溜		bīngliù	icicle
拖		tuō	to drag, to pull

手提箱		shǒutíxiāng	small suitcase
移動	移动	yídòng	to move
泥		ní	mud
圈		quān	circle, ring
圍觀	围观	wéiguān	to gather around and watch
輕微	轻微	qīngwēi	slight
朝陽	朝阳	zhāoyáng	the morning sun
輕浮	轻浮	qīngfú	light and as floating
瀰漫	弥漫	mímàn	to fill the air, to spread all over the place
碎		suì	broken, fragmentary
剛強	刚强	gāngqiáng	firm, staunch, unyielding
刺痛		cìtòng	to sting, to pierce

手

词语例句

一、连…也…，何况…   even …, not to mention …

※ 他说连小店进去喝一碗水也多少得赏点钱，何况学堂呢?

1. 在中国，连上厕所都要钱，何况参观博物馆呢?

2. 他连中国电影都看不懂，何况中文报纸呢?

二、多少…   more or less

※ 连喝一碗水多少也得赏点钱，何况学堂呢?

1. 他既然是个学者，多少也得有点学问吧?

2. 他又忘了妻子的生日，妻子虽不在乎,但多少有点失望。

三、如同…似的   好像…似的

※ 看那样子，她好像是害怕，就如同让她去接触黑色的已经死掉的鸟类似的。

1. 他不停地说话，如同不这样就不能证明他还存在似的。

2. 新年夜的广场灯火通明，如同大白天似的。

四、至于   as for

※ …至于她的肩头一点也不再显出蛮野和强壮。

1. 他看上去无忧无虑，至于他内心想什么就不得而知了。

2. 说中文不难，至于写中国字就不容易了。

五、…还不说，…   to leave … aside; besides

※ 两只蓝手还不说，你看看你这件上衣，快变成灰的了!

1. 这孩子，逃学还不说，又染上了毒瘾，真让人担心!

2. 真倒霉! 吃了罚单还不说，车也给拖走了。

六、...居多　　　　　　　　　　　（＝多半儿），to be in the majority

　　※　送来染的都是大衣裳居多。

　　1．这所大学的学生是有钱人家的孩子居多。

　　2．老年人居多的现象是生育政策所导致的。

七、好像...一般　　　　　　　　　　　　　　　好像...似的

　　※　从窗子看去，人也好像和影子一般轻浮。

　　1．爬到半山腰时，人好像在雾里行走一般。

　　2．年轻人做事好像不知道有困难一般。

（八）

《呐喊》自序

呐喊		nàhǎn	to shout loudly, to cry out
自序		zìxù	author's preface
忘却		wàngquè	to forget
所謂...者	所谓...者	suǒwèi...zhě	that which is called..., that which is known as...
回憶	回忆	huíyì	recollection
歡欣	欢欣	huānxīn	joyous, happy
不免		bùmiǎn	invariably, unavoidably
寂寞		jìmò	lonely
絲縷	丝缕	sīlǚ	strand, thread
牽	牵	qiān	to be attached to, to be involved with
逝		shì	to pass; to pass away
時光	时光	shíguāng	time
意味		yìwèi	meaning
苦於	苦于	kǔyú	to suffer from
來由	来由	láiyóu	reason, cause

質鋪	质铺	zhìpù	pawn shop, 當鋪
櫃台	柜台	guìtái	counter
首飾	首饰	shǒushì	jewelry
侮蔑		wǔmiè	humiliation, insult
開方	开方	kāifāng	to write out a prescription
藥引	药引	yàoyǐn	an ingredient added to enhance the efficacy of a dose of medicine
蘆根	芦根	lúgēn	reed rhizome
霜		shuāng	frost
甘蔗		gānzhè	sugar cane
蟋蟀		xīshuài	cricket
原對	原对	yuánduì	the original pair
結子	结子	jiēzǐ	to form seeds, to seed
平地木		píngdìmù	Ardisia (an herb)
亡故		wánggù	to die, to perish
小康人家		xiǎokāngrénjiā	a comfortable family
墜入	坠入	zhuìrù	to fall into
困頓	困顿	kùndùn	difficult circumstances, dire straits

途路	途路	túlù	way, path
真面目		zhēnmiànmù	true features, true colors
N			Nanking, 南京
K 學堂		K xuétáng	The Kiangnan Naval School, 江南水師學堂
仿佛		fǎngfú	it seems, as if
異路	异路	yìlù	different road
逃		táo	to escape
異地	异地	yìdì	different place
尋求	寻求	xúnqiú	to seek
川資	川资	chuānzī	traveling expenses, 路費
由...自便		yóu...zìbiàn	to do as one pleases
伊		yī	she (archaic)
情理		qínglǐ	reason, sense
應試	应试	yìngshì	to sit for examination, (here) to take the civil service examinations
正路		zhènglù	the right way, the correct path
洋務	洋务	yángwù	foreign things, foreign business
走投無路	走投无路	zǒu tóu wú lù	to have nowhere to turn to, to be at the end of one's rope

靈魂	灵魂	línghún	soul
鬼子		guǐzi	devil, foreigner
加倍		jiābèi	doubly
奚落		xīluò	to scoff at
排斥		páichì	to exclude, to reject
而況		érkuàng	moreover
顧不得	顾不得	gùbudé	to have no time to worry about
格致		gézhì	(archaic) physics, 物理
算學	算学	suànxué	(archaic) mathematics, 数学
繪圖	绘图	huìtú	drawing
體操	体操	tǐcāo	physical training; gymnastics
生理學	生理学	shēnglǐxué	physiology
木版		mùbǎn	wood block (for printing)
全體新論	全体新论	Quántǐxīnlùn	*New Treatise on the Human Body*
化學衛生論	化学卫生论	Huàxuéwèishēnglùn	*Treatise on Chemical Hygiene*
議論	议论	yìlùn	discussion, comment
方藥	方药	fāngyào	prescription

悟得		wùdé	to become aware of, to realize
有意		yǒuyì	intentionally, purposely
騙子	骗子	piànzi	swindler, cheat
日本維新	日本维新	Rìběnwéixīn	The Meiji Restoration of Japan
發端	发端	fāduān	to originate, to start
幼稚		yòuzhì	puerile, naive
學籍	学籍	xuéjí	one's status as a student
列		liè	to list, to be listed
美滿	美满	měimǎn	happy, wonderful
卒業	卒业	zúyè	to graduate
救治		jiùzhì	to treat and cure
誤	误	wù	to harm
疾苦		jíkǔ	suffering
促進	促进	cùjìn	to promote
信仰		xìnyǎng	belief; faith
教授		jiāoshòu	to teach, to instruct
微生物學	微生物学	wēishēngwùxué	microbiology

顯示	显示	xiǎnshì	to display, to demonstrate
形狀	形状	xíngzhuàng	shape, form
講義	讲义	jiǎngyì	lecture notes; (here in accordance with Japanese usage, to mean "lecture")
段落		duànluò	paragraph, convenient stopping point
映		yìng	to project on a screen
風景	风景	fēngjǐng	scenery, landscape
時事	时事	shíshì	current events
畫片	画片	huàpiàn	pictures
多餘	多余	duōyú	extra, surplus
光陰	光阴	guāngyīn	time
日俄戰爭	日俄战争	Rì'èzhànzhēng	the Russo-Japanese War (1904-1905)
隨喜	随喜	suíxǐ	to join in the merriment
拍手		pāishǒu	to clap one's hands, to applaud
喝采		hècǎi	to cheer
會見	会见	huìjiàn	to meet with (somebody)
久違	久违	jiǔwéi	to have not seen for a long time
綁	绑	bǎng	to tie, to bind

强壮	强壮	qiángzhuàng	strong
體格	体格	tǐgé	physique
顯出	显出	xiǎnchū	to exhibit; to appear
麻木		mámù	numb
神情		shénqíng	facial expression
解説	解说	jiěshuō	explanation
軍事	军事	jūnshì	military
偵探	侦探	zhēntàn	spy
砍		kǎn	to cut, to hack
頭顱	头颅	tóulú	head
示衆	示众	shìzhòng	to exhibit to the public
圍		wéi	to surround, to encircle
賞鑒	赏鉴	shǎngjiàn	to examine and appreciate
盛舉	盛举	shèngjǔ	magnificent event, worthy undertaking
學年	学年	xuénián	academic year
東京	东京	Dōngjīng	Tokyo
愚弱		yúruò	stupid and weak

健全		jiànquán	healthy, in good shape
茁壯	茁壮	zhuózhuàng	strong, vigorous
材料		cáiliào	material
看客		kànkè	watcher, onlooker
要着		yàozhuó	important move
善於	善于	shànyú	to be good at
推		tuī	to recommend, to single out
文藝	文艺	wényì	literature and art
法政理化		fǎ zhèng lǐ huà	law, politics, physics, and chemistry
治		zhì	to study; to research
美術	美术	měishù	fine art
冷淡		lěngdàn	indifferent
空氣	空气	kōngqì	atmosphere
同志		tóngzhì	kindred spirit; comrade
邀集		yāojí	to invite to a gathering
名目		míngmù	title
取		qǔ	to choose; to take

大抵		dàdǐ	generally speaking
復古	复古	fùgǔ	to revive ancient things
傾向	倾向	qīngxiàng	tendency
出版		chūbǎn	to publish
接近		jiējìn	to approach
隱去	隐去	yǐnqù	to disappear from sight
若干		ruògān	several, some
擔當	担当	dāndāng	to undertake
資本	资本	zīběn	capital
不名一錢	不名一钱	bù míng yì qián	without a penny to one's name
創始	创始	chuàngshǐ	to found
背時	背时	bèishí	out of touch or can't cope with the current trend
無可告語	无可告语	wú kě gào yǔ	to have nowhere to turn to
運命	运命	yùnmìng	fate
驅策	驱策	qūcè	to drive, to spur on
縱談	纵谈	zòngtán	to speak freely, to talk without inhibition
結局	结局	jiéjú	outcome

未嘗	未尝	wèicháng	have not; did not
無聊	无聊	wúliáo	ennui; boredom
不知其所以然		bù zhī qí suǒ yǐ rán	not knowing why it is so
贊和	赞和	zànhè	approval; support
促		cù	to urge, to hasten
奮鬥	奋斗	fèndòu	to fight, to struggle
生人		shēngrén	stranger
反應	反应	fǎnyìng	reaction; to react
置身		zhìshēn	to place oneself
邊際	边际	biānjì	bound, boundary
荒原		huāngyuán	wasteland, wilderness
無可措手	无可措手	wú kě cuò shǒu	unable to do anything about it
悲哀		bēi'āi	sad
毒蛇		dúshé	poisonous snake
纏住	缠住	chánzhù	to entwine
無端	无端	wúduān	for no reason, without cause
憤懣	愤懑	fènmèn	depressed and discontented

反省		fǎnxǐng	to examine oneself, to question oneself
振臂一呼應者雲集 振臂一呼应者云集		zhèn bì yī hū yìng zhě yún jí	one raises his arms and issues a call to action; the multitude hears and follows
英雄		yīngxióng	hero
驅除	驱除	qūchú	to get rid of, to drive out
麻醉		mázuì	to numb; to anaesthetize
沉入		chénrù	to sink into
親歷	亲历	qīnlì	to personally experience
旁觀	旁观	pángguān	to observe, to look on
追懷	追怀	zhuīhuái	to recall
甘心		gānxīn	to be willing to
消滅	消灭	xiāomiè	to perish, to die out
泥土		nítǔ	earth, soil
奏功		zòugōng	to be effective, to be successful
慷慨激昂		kāngkǎi jī'áng	impassioned, vehement
S			Shaoxing, 紹興
會館	会馆	huìguǎn	guild hall, provincial or county guild
相傳	相传	xiāngchuán	the story goes that ...

往昔		wǎngxī	in the past
槐樹	槐树	huáishù	locust tree
縊	缢	yì	to hang; to strangle
攀		pān	to reach up
寓		yù	to reside, to live
抄		chāo	to copy by hand
古碑		gǔbēi	ancient stone inscriptions
客中		kèzhōng	away from place of family origin, on the road
願望	愿望	yuànwàng	wish, aspiration
蒲扇		púshàn	cattail leaf fan
密		mì	dense, thick
縫	缝	fèng	a crack, an opening
蠶	蚕	cán	silkworm
頭頸	头颈	tóujǐng	neck
偶或		ǒuhuò	occasionally
長衫	长衫	chángshān	long gown
心房		xīnfáng	heart (physical organ)

怦怦		pēngpēng	to go pit-a-pat
翻		fān	to flip through
抄本		chāoběn	handwritten copy
質問	质问	zhìwèn	interrogation
不特		bútè	not only, 不但
許是	许是	xǔshì	也許是
萬難	万难	wànnán	extremely difficult
破毀		pòhuǐ	to ruin, to destroy
熟睡		shúshuì	to sleep soundly
悶死	闷死	mēnsǐ	to die of suffocation
昏睡		hūnshuì	drowsiness
就死		jiùsǐ	to go to one's death
大嚷		dàrǎng	to shout loudly
驚起	惊起	jīngqǐ	to wake up with a start
清醒		qīngxǐng	clear-headed, sober
挽救		wǎnjiù	to save, to rescue
臨終	临终	línzhōng	the moment before death

苦楚		kǔchǔ	pain, agony
毀壞	毁坏	huǐhuài	to destroy
確信	确信	quèxìn	firm conviction
抹殺	抹杀	mǒshā	to blot out, to write off
證明	证明	zhèngmíng	proof, evidence
折服		zhéfú	to subdue, to bring into submission
狂人日記	狂人日记	Kuángrénrìjì	*A Madman's Diary*
一發而不可收		yì fā ér bù kě shōu	impossible to halt once started
一发而不可收			
模樣	模样	múyàng	appearance, look
敷衍		fūyǎn	to be perfunctory, to perform one's duty in a perfunctory manner
囑托	嘱托	zhǔtuō	to request, to entrust
積久	积久	jījiǔ	in the course of time
切迫		qièpò	pressing, eager
不能已於言	不能已于言	bù néng yǐ yú yán	to be unable to desist from speaking
忘懷	忘怀	wànghuái	to forget
聊以		liáoyǐ	just to
慰藉	慰藉	wèijiè	to comfort

奔馳	奔驰	bēnchí	to run quickly, to gallop
猛士		měngshì	brave warrior
不憚	不惮	búdàn	to not be afraid of
前驅	前驱	qiánqū	to rush forward
勇猛		yǒngměng	bold and powerful
可憎		kězēng	detestable
不暇顧及	不暇顾及	bùxiá gùjí	to have no time to worry about
將令	将令	jiànglìng	the orders of the commander
不恤		búxù	to be willing even to (do something against one's principles)
曲筆	曲笔	qūbǐ	distortion of the facts in writing
瑜兒	瑜儿	Yú'ér	personal name
墳	坟	fén	grave, tomb
憑空	凭空	píngkōng	groundlessly, without foundation
花環	花环	huāhuán	wreath
叙		xù	to narrate
單四嫂子	单四嫂子	Shànsì sǎozi	personal name
主將	主将	zhǔjiàng	commander-in-chief

消極	消极	xiāojí	pessimism, negativity
傳染	传染	chuánrǎn	to infect
藝術	艺术	yìshù	art
距離	距离	jùlí	distance
可想而知		kě xiǎng ér zhī	can be imagined
蒙着...的名		méngzhe... deming	to receive the unmerited title of
成集		chéngjí	to be collected into a volume
僥倖	侥幸	jiǎoxìng	lucky
不安於心	不安于心	bù ān yú xīn	uneasy in one's mind
懸揣	悬揣	xuánchuǎi	to guess, to conjecture
暫時	暂时	zànshí	for the moment, for the time being
短篇小説	短篇小说	duǎnpiān xiǎoshuō	short story
結集	结集	jiéjí	to collect together
付印		fùyìn	to send to the press
緣由	缘由	yuányóu	reason, cause
稱	称	chēng	to call

《呐喊》自序
词语例句

一、所谓…者，…   that which is called …

※所谓回忆者，虽说可以使人欢欣，有时也不免使人寂寞。

1．所谓说谎者，虽然可恶，有时却是善意的。

2．所谓困难者，也是因人而异的。

二、不免   unavoidably

※ 所谓回忆者，虽说可以使人欢欣，有时也不免使人寂寞。

1．实验的失败不免使人失望。

2．酒后驾车不免出车祸。

三、偏（偏）   contrary to what is expected

※ 而我偏苦于不能全忘却。

1．节日期间人人都兴高采烈，他偏偏愁眉不展。

2．今天有晚会，我却偏偏忙于论文而不能参加。

四、仿佛   it seems，as if

※ 我要到N进K学堂去了，仿佛是想走异路，逃异地，去寻求别样的
    人们。

1．他头也不回地走了，好像什么也没有发生过。

2．他去了非洲，仿佛是要寻找一种新的生活。

五、由…自便   to do as one pleases

※ 我的母亲没有法，…说是由我的自便。

1．他要学什么都行，由他自便吧。

2．老师这次没有规定作文题，由学生自便。

六、起了对于…的（abstract noun） 对…产生了…

※ …同时又很起了对于被骗的病人和他的家族的同情。

1. 看了那篇报导，很起了对于被害人的怜悯。

2. 听了新闻以后，人们起了对于政府的不满。

七、发端于 to originate from

※ 日本维新是大半发端于西方医学的。

1. 这些理论都是发端于孔孟之道的。

2. 我实在不知道他的思想发端于什么学说。

八、a clause + 以 V. … to do … in order to

※ 教师便映些风景或时事的画片给学生看，以用去这多余的光阴。

1. 有空应该多看中文电影以提高中文水平。

2. 他希望能通过这次考试，以实现作律师的愿望。

九、善于 to be good at

※ …而善于改变精神的是，我那时以为当然要推文艺。

1. 他因善于绘画而找到了一份理想的工作。

2. 他最大的问题是不善于交际。

十、…以至… and even

※ 在东京的留学生很有学法政理化以至警察工业的。

1. 美国的中级、高级以至最高法院都出面干涉了这个案子。

2. 这些孩子抽烟、喝酒以至吸毒都是无人管教的结果。

十一、带…倾向 to have … tendency

※ 我们那时大抵带些复古的倾向。

1. 这儿的演讲常带保守的倾向。

2. 各种意见都带有一定的倾向。

十二、为…所 V.　　　　　　　　　　　to be Verb-ed by

※ 这三个人也都为各自的命运所驱策，不能在一处纵谈将来的好梦了。

1．为不知道会不会发生的事所烦恼，实在不值得。

2．人很容易为这种故事所激动。

十三、不知其所以然　（know the hows but）don't know the whys

※ 我感到未尝经验的无聊，是自此以后的事。我当初是不知其所以然的。

1．人们对身边的许多事情都是不知其所以然的。

2．我已经知道了问题的答案，可还是不知其所以然。

十四、以…为…　　　　　　　　　　　to take … as …

※ 这是怎样的悲哀啊，我于是以我所感到者为寂寞。

1．我这么做当然是以友情为重。

2．中国政府目前以经济改革为主要目标。

十五、以…来 V…　　　　　　　　　　用…来…

※ 绝不能以我之必无的证明，来折服了他之所谓可有。

1．下雪天他只好以看书来消磨时间。

2．他试图以他所得出的结论来说服大家。

十六、聊以 V…　　　　　　　　　　　merely to Verb. …

※ 我有时候仍不免呐喊几声，聊以慰藉那在寂寞里奔驰的勇士。

1．我想送给他一点小礼物聊以表示我的谢意。

2．离婚后他常去酒吧，聊以消除那无边的寂寞。

(九)

九年的家鄉教育

家鄉	家乡	jiāxiāng	hometown
光緒	光绪	Guāngxù	name of period of Qing emperor Guangxu's reign (1875-1908)
調	调	diào	to transfer
台南		Táinán	city of Tainan
台東	台东	Táidōng	city of Taidong
直隸州	直隶州	zhílìzhōu	municipality directly under the Central Government
知州		zhīzhōu	mayor
草創	草创	cǎochuàng	rough to initiate, in the initial stages
故		gù	因此
家眷		jiājuàn	family (wife and children)
甲午		jiǎwǔ	the name of the year 1894 in the traditional counting system
戰事	战事	zhànshì	war
備戰	备战	bèizhàn	to make war preparations
區域	区域	qūyù	area
恰好		qiàhǎo	to so happen that, to happen coincidentally that

112

托		tuō	to request (that someone does something).
故鄉	故乡	gùxiāng	hometown
正月		zhēngyuè	the first month of the lunar year
起程		qǐchéng	to set out
績溪	绩溪	Jīxī	Jixi County
和議	和议	héyì	agreement
割讓	割让	gēràng	to cede (territory)
西洋		xīyáng	Western countries
干涉		gānshè	to interfere
不允		bùyǔn	to not consent to
巡撫	巡抚	xúnfǔ	the title of a Qing Government official
唐景崧		Táng Jǐngsōng	name of a person
幫辦軍務	帮办军务	bāngbànjūnwù	military attaché
劉永福	刘永福	Líu Yǒngfú	name of a person
主軍	主军	zhǔjūn	chief commander
腳氣病	脚气病	jiǎoqìbìng	beriberi
閏月	闰月	rùnyuè	intercalary month in the lunar calendar

安平		Ānpíng	name of a port in Southern Taiwan
苦苦		kǔkǔ	persistently
放行		fàngxíng	to allow to leave
厦門	厦门	Xiàmén	city of Xiamen
手足		shǒuzú	手腳
俱		jù	都
犧牲	牺牲	xīshēng	to sacrifice
仿佛		fǎngfú	as if
門檻	门槛	ménkǎn	threshold
珍伯母		Zhēn Bómǔ	Aunt Zhen
翻覆	翻覆	fānfù	to turn upside-down
凄慘	凄惨	qīcǎn	miserable
情狀	情状	qíngzhuàng	situation
其餘	其余	qíyú	the rest
馮氏	冯氏	Féngshì	Ms. Feng
遭亂	遭乱	zāoluàn	to meet with chaos
太平天國	太平天国	Tàipíngtiānguó	the Taiping Heavenly Kingdom (1851-1864)

兵亂	兵乱	bīngluàn	turmoil of war
次		cì	the second; then
曹氏		Cáoshì	Ms. Cao
續娶	续娶	xùqǔ	to remarry (a woman)
江蘇	江苏	Jiāngsū	Jiangsu province
稍稍		shāoshāo	a bit
嗣稼		Sìjià	name of a person
娶親	娶亲	qǔqīn	(of a man) to get married
出嫁		chūjià	(of a woman) to get married
後母	后母	hòumǔ	stepmother
免不了		miǎnbùliǎo	to be unable to avoid
脫離	脱离	tuōlí	to leave from
鍾愛	钟爱	zhōng'ài	to cherish
滿...歲	满...岁	mǎn...suì	to be... full years old
溫		wēn	to review
熟字		shúzì	words learned
代理		dàilǐ	substitute

近		jìn	nearly
楷字		kǎizì	regular script (in Chinese calligraphy)
終身	终身	zhōngshēn	in one's entire life
保存		bǎocún	to keep, to preserve
神聖	神圣	shénshèng	sacred
團居	团居	tuánjū	to live together
紀念	纪念	jìniàn	memento, commemoration
寡婦	寡妇	guǎfù	widow
含辛茹苦		hánxīnrúkǔ	to endure all kinds of hardships
寄托		jìtuō	to place (hope) on
渺茫		miǎománg	uncertain; vague
掙扎		zhēngzhá	to struggle
臨V.	临V.	lín V.	just before V...
遺囑	遗嘱	yízhǔ	written will
天資	天资	tiānzī	natural talent
頗	颇	pō	很
上進	上进	shàngjìn	to make progress, to improve

寥寥		liáoliáo	few
冷笑		lěngxiào	to sneer
始終	始终	shǐzhōng	from beginning to end; the entire time
忍氣	忍气	rěnqì	to swallow one's anger
得罪		dézuì	to offend
財政	财政	cáizhèng	finance
若		ruò	要是
供給	供给	gōngjǐ	to provide
學費	学费	xuéfèi	tuition
終	终	zhōng	after all
況且		kuàngqiě	moreover
隔		gé	after; at an interval of
肺病		fèibìng	pulmonary tuberculosis
弱		ruò	weak
號稱	号称	hàochēng	to be known as
跨		kuà	to step over; to stride
寸		cùn	a unit of length

切		qiè	anxious
介如		Jièrú	name of a person
學堂	学堂	xuétáng	school
四書	四书	Sìshū	The Four Books
詩經	诗经	Shījīng	The Book of Songs
書經	书经	Shūjīng	The Book of History
易經	易经	Yìjīng	The Book of Changes
禮記	礼记	Lǐjì	The Book of Rites
論語	论语	Lúnyǔ	The Analects of Confucius
家塾		jiāshú	old style private school
移交		yíjiāo	to turn over to
族兄		zúxiōng	clan brother
禹臣		Yǔchén	name of a person
添		tiān	to increase
蒙館	蒙馆	méngguǎn	old style private school
學金	学金	xuéjīn	tuition
銀元	银元	yínyuán	silver dollar

耐心		nàixīn	patience
毫不		háobù	一點都不
趣味		qùwèi	interest
逃學	逃学	táoxué	to cut class
捉		zhuō	to capture
屬於	属于	shǔyú	to belong to
階級	阶级	jiējí	social class
渴望		kěwàng	to hope; to long for
優厚	优厚	yōuhòu	munificent, generous
叮囑	叮嘱	dīngzhǔ	to urge again and again
囑托	嘱托	zhǔtuō	to entrust
臥房		wòfáng	bedroom
偶然		ǒurán	by chance
板箱		bǎnxiāng	wooden suitcase
廢紙堆	废纸堆	fèizhǐduī	pile of waste paper
露出		lùchū	to stick out (visually); to reveal
老鼠		lǎoshǔ	mouse

開闢	开辟	kāipì	to open up
新鮮	新鲜	xīnxiān	new; fresh
水滸傳	水浒传	Shuǐhǔzhuàn	*The Water Margin,* by Shi Nai'an
李逵	李逵	Lǐ Kuí	a character in *The Water Margin*
殷天錫	殷天锡	Yīn Tiānxī	a character in *The Water Margin*
一回		yīhuí	one chapter
戲台	戏台	xìtái	stage
一口氣	一口气	yīkǒuqì	without stopping
殘本	残本	cánběn	incomplete copy
尚可		shàngkě	還可以
不料		búliào	to one's surprise
守焕		Shǒuhuàn	name of a person
三國演義	三国演义	Sānguóyǎnyì	*The Romance of The Three Kingdoms* by Luo Guanzhong
鄭重	郑重	zhèngzhòng	seriously
捧		pěng	to hold in both hands
薛仁貴	薛仁贵	Xuē Rénguì	name of a person
征		zhēng	to go on an expedition

紅樓夢	紅楼梦	Hónglóumèng	*Dream of The Red Chamber* by Cao Xueqin
儒林外史		Rúlínwàishǐ	*The Scholars* by Wu Jingzi
作品		zuòpǐn	written works
程度		chéngdù	level
天懸地隔	天悬地隔	tiān xuán dì gé	to differ tremendously
白話	白话	báihuà	vernacular
不知不覺	不知不觉	bù zhī bù jué	unwittingly
散文		sǎnwén	prose
訓練	训练	xùnliàn	practice, training
尚書	尚书	Shàngshū	書經
通順文字	通顺文字	tōngshùn wénzì	coherent writing
絕大	绝大	juédà	great, considerable
細細地	细细地	xìxìde	attentively
本家		běnjiā	people of the same clan/family
聊齋	聊斋	Liáozhāi	*Strange Stories from a Chinese Studio* by Pu Songling
繡花	绣花	xiùhuā	to do embroidery
逼		bī	to force

土話	土话	tǔhuà	local dialect
文理		wénlǐ	logic and grammar
像樣	像样	xiàngyàng	presentable
究竟		jiūjìng	after all, in the final analysis
恩師	恩师	ēnshī	benefactor; teacher
慈母		címǔ	loving mother
披		pī	to throw on (clothes); to drape across one's shoulders
清醒		qīngxǐng	clear-headed
踏		tà	to follow; to step on
脚步		jiǎobù	footsteps
曉得	晓得	xiǎode	知道
丟...的臉	丢...的脸	diū...deliǎn	to make somebody ashamed
催		cuī	to urge; to hurry (someone)
管束		guǎnshù	to keep under strict control
兼		jiān	and
嚴厲	严厉	yánlì	stern
嚇	吓	xià	to scare

犯		fàn	to violate, to commit
静		jìng	quiet
責備	责备	zébèi	to reproach
行罰	行罚	xíngfá	to carry out punishment
罰跪	罚跪	fáguì	to punish with kneeling
擰	拧	níng	to pinch
教訓	教训	jiàoxùn	to teach a lesson, to reprimand
當家	当家	dāngjiā	to manage (household) affairs
寬裕	宽裕	kuānyù	comfortably off
經營	经营	jīngyíng	to manage
調度	调度	diàodù	to adjust; to control
敗家子	败家子	bàijiāzǐ	wastrel, prodigal son
鴉片	鸦片	yāpiàn	opium
賭博	赌博	dǔbó	to gamble
打主意		dǎzhǔyì	to scheme (to get something)
值錢	值钱	zhíqián	valuable
當	当	dàng	to pawn, to hock

邀		yāo	to invite
長輩	长辈	zhǎngbèi	elder (senior) member of a family
欠債	欠债	qiànzhài	to owe a debt
除夕		chúxī	New Year's Eve
討債	讨债	tǎozhài	to demand payment of a debt
燈籠	灯笼	dēnglóng	lantern
大廳	大厅	dàtīng	front hall
避		bì	to escape
債主	债主	zhàizhǔ	creditor
料理		liàolǐ	to take care of, to arrange
年夜飯	年夜饭	niányèfàn	New Year's Eve dinner
灶神		Zàoshén	Kitchen God
壓歲錢	压岁钱	yāsuìqián	money given to children as a New Year's gift
鄰舍	邻舍	línshè	neighbouring
債戶	债户	zhàihù	債主
開發	开发	kāifā	to hand out, to pass out
說好說歹	说好说歹	shuō hǎo shuō dǎi	to say whatever it takes

124

敲門	敲门	qiāomén	to knock at the door
露出		lùchū	to show, to reveal
怒色		nùsè	anger, wrath
嫂		sǎo	(older) sister-in-law
無能	无能	wúnéng	incompetent
懂事		dǒngshì	sensible
氣量窄小	气量窄小	qìliàng zhǎixiǎo	narrow-minded
鬧意見	闹意见	nào yìjiàn	to be on bad terms because of differing opinions, to bicker
和氣	和气	héqì	polite
榜樣	榜样	bǎngyàng	model
公然		gōngrán	openly
相打相罵	相打相骂	xiāng dǎ xiāng mà	to fight and insult each other
把臉板起來	把脸板起来	bǎ liǎn bǎnqǐlái	to put on a stern face
青		qīng	green or blue
如此		rúcǐ	像這樣
起初		qǐchū	at first
套		tào	AN for stereotyped things

125

漸漸	渐渐	jiànjiàn	gradually
世間	世间	shìjiān	in this world
厭惡	厌恶	yànwù	disgusting
莫如		mòrú	nothing is more ... than
下流		xiàliú	mean, obscene
擺	摆	bǎi	to put on (an expression)
性子		xìngzi	disposition
婆		pó	mother-in -law
留心		liúxīn	to be careful
格外		géwài	especially, all the more
容忍		róngrěn	to tolerate
飲食	饮食	yǐnshí	food
衣料		yīliào	clothing
爭執	争执	zhēngzhí	dispute
吃虧	吃亏	chīkuī	to get the worst of it
尖刻		jiānkè	biting, acrimonious (words)
刺		cì	thorn, sting

裝作	裝作	zhuāngzuò	to pretend
忍不住		rěnbuzhù	to be unable to bear
悄悄		qiāoqiāo	quietly
吵嘴		chǎozuǐ	to quarrel
仁慈		réncí	kind, merciful
温和		wēnhé	gentle
傷感情	伤感情	shāng gǎnqíng	to hurt one's feelings
剛氣	刚气	gāngqì	upright and unyielding
人格		rén'gé	human dignity
侮辱		wǔrǔ	to humiliate; humiliation
無正業	无正业	wúzhèngyè	vagrant
烟館	烟馆	yānguǎn	opium house
發牢騷	发牢骚	fā láosāo	to grumble
當面	当面	dāngmiàn	face to face
質問	质问	zhìwèn	to question bluntly
直到		zhídào	until
當衆	当众	dāngzhòng	in public

認錯	认错	rèncuò	to admit a fault
賠罪	赔罪	péizuì	to apologize
罷休	罢休	bàxiū	to let the matter drop
廣漠	广漠	guǎngmò	vast and bare
獨自	独自	dúzì	alone
混		hùn	to drift along
一絲一毫	一丝一毫	yì sī yì háo	a tiny bit
脾氣	脾气	píqì	temper
待人接物		dài rén jiē wù	to deal with things and people
寬恕	宽恕	kuānshù	to forgive
體諒	体谅	tǐliàng	to be understanding

九年的家乡教育
词语例句

一、免不了　　　　　　　　　　　　　　　　　　　unavoidable

※ 这样一个家庭里，...她的生活免不了苦痛。

1. 所有的朋友都弃他而去，他免不了难过。

2. 无家可归者免不了挨冻受饿。

二、临V. ...　　　　　　　　　　　　　　　　　just before V. ...

※ 我父亲在临死之前两个多月，写了几张遗嘱，每张只有几句话。

1. 这种药是临睡前吃的。

2. 他临去中国之前还来看过我。

三、究竟　　　　　　　　　　　　　　　　　　　　　after all

※ 但父亲的遗嘱究竟是父亲的遗嘱，我是应该念书的。

1. 我在这九年之中，除了读书之外，究竟也受到了一点做人的训练。

2. 生活虽然艰苦，孩子们究竟还是长大了。

3. 干坏事的人究竟会受到惩罚。

四、（不 V. ...）尚可　　　　　　　　　　　　　　　还可以

※ 不看尚可，看了之后，我的心里很不好过。

1. 这种烟不吸尚可，吸了就上瘾。

2. 不提那件事尚可，一提起他就忿忿不平。

五、居然　　　　　　　　　　　　　　　　　　　　surprisingly

※ 后来我居然得着《水浒》全部，《三国演义》也看完了。

1. 我们历史课的教授居然没听说过毛泽东。

2. 他居然把跟女朋友的约会给忘了。

六、于...很有用处   对...很有用处

※ 我在不知不觉中得了不少白话散文的训练，在十几年后于我很有
用处。

1. 只要不断地练习早晚会于你有用处的。

2. 不管于我有没有用处我都要坚持到底。

七、当作   to pretend to

※ 我母亲走进走出，只当作不曾看见这群人。

1. 为了不被别人发现，我只当作不认识他，从他身边走过。

2. 别紧张，你只当作什么也没发生就行了。

八、莫如   nothing is more ... than

※ 我渐渐明白，世间最可厌恶的事莫如一张生气的脸，世间最下流
的事莫如把生气的脸摆给旁人看。

1. 对学生来说，最快乐的事莫如得 A。

2. 一个人最大的痛苦莫如无家可归。

九、格外   especially

※ 我母亲因为作了后母后婆，事事格外容忍。

1. 他因得了奖而格外自豪。

2. 他今天显得格外轻松。

（十）

毛澤東的童年

毛澤東	毛泽东	Máo Zédōng	Mao Zedong
<u>童年</u>		tóngnián	childhood
湘潭縣	湘潭县	Xiāngtán xiàn	Xiangtan County
上七都		Shàngqī dū	Shangqi city
清溪鄉	清溪乡	Qīngxī xiāng	Qingxi town
韶山衝	韶山冲	Sháoshān chōng	Shaoshan village
<u>山清水秀</u>		shān qīng shuǐ xiù	green hills and clear waters
村子		cūnzi	a village
稀稀落落		xīxīluòluò	sparse; thinly scattered
孫	孙	Sūn	(surname)
鄒	邹	Zōu	(surname)
彭		Péng	(surname)
郭		Guō	(surname)
龐	庞	Páng	(surname)
蔣	蒋	Jiǎng	(surname)

務農	务农	wùnóng	to farm
忠厚		zhōnghòu	honest and sincere
樸實	朴实	pǔshí	simple and plain
勤勞	勤劳	qínláo	hardworking and diligent
善良		shànliáng	kindhearted
公曆	公历	gōnglì	公元 -- the Christian era
清		Qīng	Qing Dynasty
光緒	光绪	Guāngxù	the title of a Qing emperor's reign (1875-1908)
陰曆	阴历	yīnlì	lunar calendar
癸		guǐ	the last of the ten Heavenly Stems
巳		sì	the sixth of the twelve Earthly Branches
本		běn	本來
貧農	贫农	pínnóng	a poor peasant
身材		shēncái	stature; figure
晚年		wǎnnián	old age
蓄		xù	to grow; to wear (a beard)
體格	体格	tǐgé	physique

個性	个性	gèxìng	personality
強健	强健	qiángjiàn	strong and healthy
勤儉	勤俭	qínjiǎn	industrious and thrifty
爲人	为人	wéirén	to conduct oneself
精明		jīngmíng	shrewd; astute
善於	善於	shànyú	to be good at ...
經管	经管	jīngguǎn	to be in charge of
家務	家务	jiāwù	household duties
負債	负债	fùzhài	to be in debt
當兵	当兵	dāngbīng	to serve in the army
家鄉	家乡	jiāxiāng	hometown
省		shěng	to economize; to live frugally
積	积	jī	to save
畝	亩	mǔ	a unit of area (=0.0667 hectares)
耕種	耕种	gēngzhòng	to cultivate
中農	中农	zhōngnóng	middle peasant
澤民	泽民	Zémín	a brother of Mao Zedong

憑	凭	píng	by; to use
食用		shíyòng	吃的和用的
剩餘	剩馀	shèngyú	remainder
資本	资本	zīběn	capital
添		tiān	to add
澤覃	泽覃	Zétán	a brother of Mao Zedong
家產	家产	jiāchǎn	family property
販運	贩运	fànyùn	to transport goods for sale
穀米	谷米	gǔmǐ	unhusked rice
豬		zhū	pig
富農	富农	fùnóng	rich peasant
勞動	劳动	láodòng	to work, to labor
資本主義	资本主义	zīběnzhǔyì	capitalism
帝國主義	帝国主义	dìguózhǔyì	imperialism
加緊	加紧	jiājǐn	to speed up; to intensify
擴張	扩张	kuòzhāng	to expand
侵略	侵略	qīnlüè	to invade

閉關自守	闭关自守	bìguān zìshǒu	to close the country to international intercourse
事實上	事实上	shìshíshàng	in fact
洋槍	洋枪	yángqiāng	foreign guns
大炮		dàpào	artillery; cannon
米突尺		mǐtūchǐ	the metric ruler
十字架		shízìjià	cross
即		jí	也就是, namely, that is
軍事	军事	jūnshì	military
衝倒	冲倒	chōngdǎo	to crush
誕生	诞生	dànshēng	to be born
鴉片	鸦片	yāpiàn	opium
戰爭	战争	zhànzhēng	war
經受	经受	jīngshòu	to suffer
訂立	订立	dìnglì	to sign into effect
平等		píngděng	even, equal
條約	条约	tiáoyuē	treaty
喪失	丧失	sàngshī	to lose; to forfeit

獨立自主	独立自主	dúlì zìzhǔ	to be independent and act on one's own
主權	主权	zhǔquán	sovereign rights
領土	领土	lǐngtǔ	territory
劃分	划分	huàfēn	to carve out
勢力	势力	shìlì	influence
範圍	范围	fànwéi	sphere
文明		wénmíng	civilization
逐漸	逐渐	zhújiàn	gradually
任人宰割		rèn rén zǎi gē	to allow oneself to be oppressed and exploited
半殖民地		bànzhímíndì	semi-colony
面臨	面临	miànlín	to confront, to face
列強		lièqiáng	big powers
瓜分		guāfēn	to carve up
光景		guāngjǐng	時間
貨物	货物	huòwù	goods
廣東	广东	Guǎngdōng	Guangdong Province
岸		àn	river bank

內地		nèidì	inland, interior
絲茶	丝茶	sīchá	silk and tea leaves
裝箱	装箱	zhuāngxiāng	to pack (a box)
廣州	广州	Guǎngzhōu	Guangzhou
放洋		fàngyáng	to ship abroad
商務	商务	shāngwù	business
繁盛		fánshèng	prosperous
陸路	陆路	lùlù	to travel by land; land route
肩貨	肩货	jiānhuò	to shoulder goods
不下		búxià	as many as; no less than
處在	处在	chǔzài	to be in (a certain condition)
辛苦		xīnkǔ	hard work
經營	经营	jīngyíng	to manage; to build up
建立		jiànlì	to establish
新興	新兴	xīnxīng	burgeoning; developing
氣象	气象	qìxiàng	atmosphere
主人		zhǔrén	master

家長	家长	jiāzhǎng	head of a family
精力		jīnglì	energy
寧都	宁都	Níngdū	Ningdu county
寧田市	宁田市	Níngtián shì	Ningtian city
長沙	长沙	Chángshā	Changsha city
僱	雇	gù	to hire
長工	长工	chánggōng	long-term hired hand
田地		tiándì	field
農忙	农忙	nóngmáng	busy season (in farming)
插秧		chāyāng	to transplant rice seedlings
踹田		chuàitián	to tread the field
秋收		qiūshōu	autumn harvest
打稻		dǎdào	to thresh rice
零工		línggōng	odd-job man
妻室		qīshì	wife
磨米		mòmǐ	to grind rice
臨時	临时	línshí	temporarily

短工		duǎngōng	short-term hired hand; laborer
便		biàn	就
節省	节省	jiéshěng	to be economical, thrifty
成年人		chéngniánrén	adult
記賬	记账	jìzhàng	to keep accounts
學問	学问	xuéwèn	knowledge
月亮		yuèliàng	the moon
打算盤	打算盘	dǎ suànpán	to calculate on an abacus
糙米飯	糙米饭	cāomǐfàn	(cooked) coarse rice, generally eaten by the poor
蔬菜		shūcài	vegetables
逢		féng	on (a specific day)
初一		chūyī	the first day of a lunar month
僱工	雇工	gùgōng	hired laborers
類	类	lèi	type; kind
群衆	群众	qúnzhòng	the masses
農家子	农家子	nóngjiāzǐ	a farmer's son
出身		chūshēn	economic, family and class background

密切		mìqiè	close, intimate
聯繫	联系	liánxì	connection, link
誠實	诚实	chéngshí	honest
唐家坨		Tángjiātuó	Tangjiatuo town
中等		zhōngděng	medium
方正		fāngzhèng	square-shaped
面龐	面庞	miànpáng	face
和善		héshàn	kind and gentle
德性		déxìng	moral conduct
憐惜	怜惜	liánxī	to have pity for
每逢		měiféng	whenever
荒年		huāngnián	famine year
旱月		hànyuè	months of drought
背着		bèizhe	behind the back of
施捨	施舍	shīshě	to give alms
饑餓	饥饿	jī'è	hungry; starving
賢良	贤良	xiánliáng	virtuous

治家		zhìjiā	to manage a household
節儉	节俭	jiéjiǎn	frugality
撫養	抚养	fǔyǎng	to raise; to bring up
兒輩	儿辈	érbèi	children
農婦	农妇	nóngfù	peasant woman
拾柴		shíchái	to collect firewood
紡棉	纺棉	fǎngmián	to spin and weave
縫補	缝补	féngbǔ	to sew and mend
漿洗	浆洗	jiāngxǐ	to wash and starch
孝		xiào	to be filial to
一貫	一贯	yíguàn	all along, consistently
溫順	温顺	wēnshùn	docile, meek
體貼入微	体贴入微	tǐtiērùwēi	to show deep love and concern
美德		měidé	moral excellence
傳說	传说	chuánshuō	to be on people's lips
時節	时节	shíjié	season
稻穀	稻谷	dàogǔ	paddy

攤	摊	tān	to spread out
坪		píng	level sunning ground
曬	晒	shài	to dry in the sun
幼年		yòunián	young; child
佃戶		diànhù	tenant peasant
交租		jiāozū	to pay the land rent
損失	损失	sǔnshī	to lose
遇		yù	to meet
風雪	风雪	fēngxuě	wind and snow
單衣	单衣	dānyī	unlined garment
凍	冻	dòng	to freeze
發抖	发抖	fādǒu	to shiver, to shake
外套		wàitào	jacket, overcoat
檢查	检查	jiǎnchá	to examine
照實	照实	zhàoshí	based on fact
舊曆	旧历	jiùlì	lunar calendar
襤褸	褴褛	lánlǚ	ragged; shabby

可憐	可怜	kělián	poor, pitiful
現錢	现钱	xiànqián	cash
好學	好学	hàoxué	to enjoy learning
私塾		sīshú	old-style private school
經書	经书	jīngshū	Confucian classics
對於	对於	duìyú	to, for
枯燥		kūzào	dry and uninteresting
無味	无味	wúwèi	boring
極點	极点	jídiǎn	the extreme
教授法		jiāoshòufǎ	teaching method
死記	死记	sǐjì	mechanical memorizing
背誦	背诵	bèisòng	to recite from memory
莫名其妙		mò míng qí miào	to be baffled
似乎		sìhū	to seem
流行		liúxíng	prevalent; popular
西遊記	西游记	Xīyóujì	*Journey to the West,* by Wu Cheng'en
封神演義	封神演义	Fēngshényǎnyì	a compilation of folk stories by Xu Zhonglin

稍		shāo	a little; a bit
水滸傳	水浒传	Shuǐhǔzhuàn	*The Water Margin*, by Shi Nai'an
藏		cáng	to hide
蓋住	盖住	gàizhù	to cover
雜書	杂书	záshū	miscellaneous (inferior) books
責備	责备	zébèi	to scold
人物		rénwù	character
講述	讲述	jiǎngshù	to tell, to narrate
則	则	zé	then
疲倦		píjuàn	tired, exhausted
經史	经史	jīngshǐ	Confucian history
再則	再则	zàizé	而且
被子		bèizi	quilt
遮住		zhēzhù	to cover up
簡陋	简陋	jiǎnlòu	simple and crude
桐油		tóngyóu	tung oil
野外		yěwài	field; open country

放牛		fàngniú	to graze cattle
樹蔭	树荫	shùyīn	shade of a tree
悠閑	悠闲	yōuxián	leisurely
出神		chūshén	to be spellbound
菜園	菜园	càiyuán	vegetable garden
發覺	发觉	fājué	to discover, to realize
亂子	乱子	luànzi	disturbance
賠償	赔偿	péicháng	to pay for; to compensate
了事		liǎoshì	to end, to get something over
壓迫	压迫	yāpò	to oppress
閱讀	阅读	yuèdú	to read
反抗		fǎnkàng	to revolt; to resist
統治階級	统治阶级	tǒngzhìjiējí	the ruling class
帝王將相	帝王将相	dì wáng jiàng xiàng	emperors, generals, and prime ministers
聖賢君子	圣贤君子	shèngxián jūnzǐ	sages, men of virtue and noble men
英雄豪傑	英雄豪杰	yīngxióng háojié	heroes and extraordinary characters
接觸	接触	jiēchù	to come into contact with

剝削		bōxuē	to exploit
懷疑	怀疑	huáiyí	doubt
自古來		zìgǔlái	since ancient times
腦子	脑子	nǎozi	brain; mind
深刻		shēnkè	deep
思想		sīxiǎng	to think
思考		sīkǎo	to consider
普遍		pǔbiàn	common; prevailing
爲...着想	为...着想	wèi...zhuóxiǎng	to consider (a person's) best interests
廣大	广大	guǎngdà	the mass of, broad
維新	维新	wéixīn	reformation
派		pài	group, school
迷信		míxìn	superstition
菩薩	菩萨	púsà	Bodhisattva
辦學堂	办学堂	bàn xuétáng	to establish a school
勸	劝	quàn	to persuade
廟産	庙产	miàochǎn	temple property

興學	兴学	xīngxué	to build schools
欽慕	钦慕	qīnmù	to admire
贊同	赞同	zàntóng	to agree
信神		xìnshén	to believe in God
關懷	关怀	guānhuái	to be concerned about
偉大	伟大	wěidà	great
行事		xíngshì	actions, behavior
愚民		yúmín	to fool people
存着		cúnzhe	to have; to harbour
心思		xīnsī	idea
倔强		juéjiàng	unbending; stubborn
嚴厲	严厉	yánlì	strict
懶惰		lǎnduò	lazy
公開	公开	gōngkāi	openly
保衛	保卫	bǎowèi	to protect
權利	权利	quánlì	rights
怯懦		qiènuò	timid and overcautious

屈服		qūfú	to surrender; to yield
凶		xiōng	fierce
鬥爭	斗争	dòuzhēng	to struggle
自衛	自卫	zìwèi	self-protection
須要	须要	xūyào	have to; need
棍子		gùnzi	stick
舊日	旧日	jiùrì	the old days
理論	理论	lǐlùn	theory
例外		lìwài	exception
打板子		dǎbǎnzi	to flog
股		gǔ	buttocks
罰跪	罚跪	fáguì	to be forced to kneel
普通		pǔtōng	ordinary
體罰	体罚	tǐfá	physical punishment
肉刑		ròuxíng	corporal punishment
消極	消极	xiāojí	passive
抵抗		dǐkàng	resistance

逃學	逃学	táoxué	to ditch school
出走		chūzǒu	to run away
挨打		áidǎ	to take a beating
方向		fāngxiàng	direction
山谷		shāngǔ	mountain valley
兜圈子		dōuquānzi	to go around in circles
不過	不过	búguò	not as many as
十來里		shíláilǐ	十幾里
終於	终于	zhōngyú	finally
出乎意料之外		chū hū yì liào zhī wài	contrary to one's expectations
暴戾		bàolì	ruthless and tyrannical
溫和		wēnhé	gentle; mild
行爲	行为	xíngwéi	behaviour
罷工	罢工	bàgōng	strike, to go on strike
勝利	胜利	shènglì	to win; to be successful
幽默		yōumò	humorous
引用		yǐnyòng	to quote

術語	术语	shùyǔ	terminology
封建		fēngjiàn	feudal
引經據典	引经据典	yǐn jīng jù diǎn	to quote the classics
辯論	辩论	biànlùn	to argue
以及		yǐjí	and
脫離	脱离	tuōlí	to break off, to leave
自殺	自杀	zìshā	suicide
以…相威脅	以…相威胁	yǐ…xiāng wēixié	to threaten with…
暴力		bàolì	tyrannous
政策		zhèngcè	policy
歸於	归于	guīyú	to result in
失敗	失败	shībài	failure
當着…面	当着…面	dāngzhe…miàn	in front of (someone)…
罪名		zuìmíng	accusation
顯然	显然	xiǎnrán	obviously
真實	真实	zhēnshí	true
冤枉		yuānwang	unjust

油鹽	油盐	yóuyán	oil and salt
不消說	不消说	bùxiāoshuō	not to mention
鹹魚	咸鱼	xiányú	salted fish
蒙		méng	to be subjected to
不服氣	不服气	bùfúqì	to feel wronged
據實	据实	jùshí	according to facts
反駁	反驳	fǎnbó	to retort; to refute
聲言	声言	shēngyán	to profess, to explain
追		zhuī	to run after
命令		mìnglìng	to command
水塘		shuǐtáng	pond
來勢	来势	láishì	the oncoming force
講和	讲和	jiǎnghé	to be reconciled
磕頭	磕头	kētóu	to kowtow
請罪	请罪	qǐngzuì	to admit one's error and ask for punishment
散		sàn	to leave; to disperse
隨着		suízhe	to follow

151

肩膀		jiānbǎng	shoulder
雙膝	双膝	shuāngxī	both knees
風暴	风暴	fēngbào	storm
平息		píngxī	to subside
從此	从此	cóngcǐ	from then on
據理力爭	据理力争	jù lǐ lì zhēng	to argue strongly on just grounds
辯護	辩护	biànhù	speak in defense of
倍		bèi	times (greater)
出力		chūlì	to exert oneself
慈		cí	loving; kind
勤勞	勤劳	qínláo	hardworking; industrious
以至		yǐzhì	to the point that, therefore
起家		qǐjiā	to make one's fortune
亦		yì	也
平價	平价	píngjià	bargain price
極	极	jí	extremely
贊成	赞成	zànchéng	to agree with

矛盾		máodùn	conflict
觀點	观点	guāndiǎn	opinion
專制	专制	zhuānzhì	tyranny, despotism
從容	从容	cōngróng	peacefully/peaceable
勸說	劝说	quànshuō	to persuade
不平		bùpíng	unfairness
刺激		cìjī	to upset; to irritate
種下	种下	zhòngxià	to plant
根		gēn	root
家長制度	家长制度	jiāzhǎngzhìdù	patriarchal system
獨裁	独裁	dúcái	dictatorship
聯合	联合	liánhé	to unite
結成	结成	jiēchéng	to form
統一戰線	统一战线	tǒngyī zhànxiàn	united front
對抗	对抗	duìkàng	to oppose
指摘		zhǐzhāi	to criticize
口實	口实	kǒushí	pretext for criticism

毛泽东的童年
词语例句

一、以...为主   to take ... as the dominant factor

  ※ 他们大都是以务农为主，忠厚朴实勤劳善良的老百姓。

  1. 美国是一个以移民为主的国家。

  2. 学校不能只顾赚钱，应该以传授知识为主。

二、凭   by, to use

  ※ 父亲凭每年食用的结余，积成资本，又买了七亩田。

  1. "棍子底下出好人"，旧日的父兄师长，就凭这个"理论"来"教育"儿童。

  2. 他凭着自己的能力当上了公司的总裁。

  3. 这种工作只凭经验是不够的。

三、凡是   every, any, all

  ※ 当时凡是外国运来的货物，到了广东上岸后，就先运到湘潭。

  1. 凡是年满十八岁的公民都有选举权。

  2. 凡是受过教育的中国人都知道鲁迅。

四、一贯   (= 一向), all along, consistently

  ※ 他对母亲是一贯温顺，体贴入微的。

  1. 他一贯省吃俭用，到退休时才买了一幢房子。

  2. 他对人一贯很和气，怎么会骂你呢?

五、一来...再则...   first ..., moreover ...

  ※ 他父亲不高兴: 一来，儿子读的不是经史，再则要节省灯油呀。

  1. 我已经决定了去北京，一来学点中文，再则也了解一点中国文化。

  2. 我打算选中文课，一来我有兴趣，再则也实用。

六、以…了事　　　　　　　　to end by …; to get sth. over by …

※ …几乎闹了一场大乱子，结果以赔偿了事。

1．他一直跟我纠缠不清，我只好以跟他道歉了事。

2．他贪污了公款，不得不以辞职了事。

七、原来　　　　　　　　　　　it turns out that …

※ 后来毛泽东发现了：原来旧小说面的人物都是一些统治者、…占了
土地叫农民替他们劳动。

1．我给你打过好几次电话都没人接，原来你去旅行了。

2．我说她们俩怎么长得那么像，原来是姐妹俩。

八、可见　　　　　　　　　it is thus clear（obvious）that …

※ 毛泽东怀疑了，发现问题了，这可见他从小就肯用脑子。

1．这么多人失业，可见经济还在继续衰退。

2．他终于成功了，可见努力总是不会白费的。

九、为…着想　　　　　　　　to consider sb's best interest

※ …他善于思考一些问题，为广大劳动人民群众着想。

1．父母总是要为子女着想的。

2．政府不为老百姓着想，为谁着想。

十、V. …，以 V. …　　　　　　to do … in order to …

※ 他找到了用"斗争"以"自卫"的办法。

1．他联合母亲、兄弟以及长工结成"统一战线"，以和压迫者对抗。

2．他花了很多时间复习以应付考试。

3．公司作了各种广告以推销产品。

十一、拿…相威胁…　　　　　　　to threaten with …

※ 他为反抗父亲的封建专制，拿脱离家庭和自杀相威胁。

1. 美国对付在政治上和她主张不同的国家的办法常常是拿经济封锁相威胁。

2. 劫机者多半是拿旅客的生命相威胁。

十二、使得…归于…　　　　　　　　to cause … to result in …

※ 他引经据典和父亲辩论，并拿脱离家庭和自杀相威胁，使得父亲的暴力政策归于失败。

1. 警察的勇敢使得恐怖分子的阴谋归于破产。

2. 新提案的目的是使得各方的意见归于一致。

十三、不消说…，就连…都/也…　　not to mention … , even …

※ …不消说吃猪肉，就连鸡蛋、咸鱼都没有得吃，怎么说是"好吃"呢?

1. 由于经济不景气，不消说一般职员，就连经理也有可能被解雇。

2. 竞选期间，不消说睡觉，就连吃饭也是有一顿没一顿的。

十四、为…辩护　　　　　　　　　　to speak in defense of

※ 父亲经常责备他懒惰和不孝，他就据理力争，为自己辩护。

1. 他没有错，所以我要尽全力为他辩护。

2. 总统总是为自己的外交政策进行辩护。

十五、以至　　　　　　　　　　therefore; with the result that

※ 父亲勤劳生产，以至起家。

1. 他一生钻研物理，以至获得诺贝尔奖。

2. 他久病不医，以至丧命。

（十一）

文學與革命

目睹		mùdǔ	親眼看見
呼聲	呼声	hūshēng	cry, voice
高唱入雲	高唱入云	gāo chàng rù yún	to sing in a very high pitch or with very great intensity -- to be very much talked about; on everybody's lips
文明		wénmíng	civilization, culture
天才		tiāncái	genius
創造	创造	chuàngzào	creation; to create
藝術	艺术	yìshù	art
聰明才智	聪明才智	cōngmíngcáizhì	intelligence, wisdom and talent
過人	过人	guòrén	超過一般的人
絲毫	丝毫	sīháo	the slightest amount
神聖	神圣	shénshèng	sacred, holy
意味		yìwèi	meaning, significance
天賦	天赋	tiānfù	natural gift, talent
厚		hòu	thick
眼光		yǎnguāng	foresight

理智		lǐzhì	reason, intellect
敏		mǐn	keen, sharp
透視	透视	tòushì	to see through
領悟	领悟	lǐngwù	to comprehend
團體	团体	tuántǐ	organization, group
結合	结合	jiéhé	group, assembly
優秀	优秀	yōuxiù	outstanding, excellent
領袖	领袖	lǐngxiù	leader
統治者	统治者	tǒngzhìzhě	ruler
依賴	依赖	yīlài	to depend on, to rely on
達到	达到	dádào	to achieve, to reach
常態	常态	chángtài	normal
路程		lùchéng	course, path
領導	领导	lǐngdǎo	to lead
任務	任务	rènwù	mission
卓越		zhuōyuè	outstanding, remarkable
謀	谋	móu	to seek

寄生蟲	寄生虫	jìshēngchóng	parasite
引導	引导	yǐndǎo	to guide
贊美	赞美	zànměi	to praise
欽佩	钦佩	qīnpèi	to admire
擁護	拥护	yōnghù	to support, to uphold
盡善	尽善	jìnshàn	perfect
盡	尽	jìn	completely
資格	资格	zīgé	qualification
平庸		píngyōng	mediocre
惡劣	恶劣	èliè	odious, abominable
世襲	世袭	shìxí	to gain (title, rank, etc.) by inheritance
強據	强据	qiángjù	to occupy by force
假		jiǎ	false, fake
貢獻	贡献	gòngxiàn	contribution
壓迫	压迫	yāpò	repression, oppression
隱	隐	yǐn	to hide, to conceal
忍無可忍	忍无可忍	rěn wú kě rěn	to be driven beyond forbearance

時機	时机	shíjī	opportune moment
指示	指示	zhǐshì	to instruct, to indicate
反抗		fǎnkàng	to resist, to revolt
變態	变态	biàntài	abnormal
目標	目标	mùbiāo	objective, target
恢復	恢复	huīfù	to regain, to restore
虛偽	虚伪	xūwěi	hypocrisy
暫時	暂时	zànshí	temporary
變動	变动	biàndòng	change, alteration
狀態	状态	zhuàngtài	state, condition
爆發	爆发	bàofā	to erupt, to break out
純粹	纯粹	chúncuì	pure
紀律	纪律	jìlù	discipline
尊重		zūnzhòng	to respect
意義	意义	yìyì	significance
上述		shàngshù	the above-mentioned
進而	进而	jìnér	further

沾染		zhānrǎn	to be infected with, to be tainted with
色彩		sècǎi	color
創作	创作	chuàngzuò	to write, to create
何以		héyǐ	why
敗壞	败坏	bàihuài	corruption, denigration
黑暗		hēi'àn	darkness; dark
深刻		shēnkè	deep, profound
知覺	知觉	zhījué	consciousness
中		zhòng	to fit exactly; to hit
繩墨	绳墨	shéngmò	(carpenter's) marking line; rule
本性		běnxìng	natural character
素養	素养	sùyǎng	one's general ability and disposition as a result of long and regular discipline
喉舌		hóushé	mouthpiece
濃烈	浓烈	nóngliè	thick and strong
直率		zhíshuài	frank, straightforward
時下	时下	shíxià	present, current
攻擊	攻击	gōngjī	attack

富於	富于	fùyú	to be rich in
想像		xiǎngxiàng	imagination
回想		huíxiǎng	to recall
黃金時代	黄金时代	huángjīnshídài	golden age
咏嘆	咏叹	yǒngtàn	to utter lofty praises about, to wax eloquent on
樂觀	乐观	lèguān	optimistic
耽於	耽于	dānyú	to indulge in
幻想		huànxiǎng	fantasy
樂園	乐园	lèyuán	paradise
一致		yízhì	unanimous
先知先覺	先知先觉	xiān zhī xiān jué	a person of foresight
觀察	观察	guānchá	to observe
與其A毋寧B 与其A毋宁B		yǔqí...wúnìng	would rather B than A
益發	益发	yìfā	all the more
鮮明	鲜明	xiānmíng	(of color) bright
近於	近于	jìnyú	to be close to
雄辯	雄辩	xióngbiàn	eloquence, convincing argument

162

宣傳	宣传	xuānchuán	propaganda
脫離	脱离	tuōlí	to break away from
刺激		cìjī	stimulus
名詞	名词	míngcí	term, phrase
成立		chénglì	to be tenable, to be able to stand up (to an argument)
立場	立场	lìchǎng	standpoint
功利		gōnglì	utility, material gain
着眼		zhuóyǎn	to view from the angle of
引申		yǐnshēn	to extend (the meaning of a word)
基於	基于	jīyú	to be based on
人性		rénxìng	human nature
潮流		cháoliú	tide, trend
理論	理论	lǐlùn	theory
拘束		jūshù	to restrain, to restrict
不相干		bùxiānggān	unrelated, irrelevant
價值	价值	jiàzhí	value, worth
軍閥	军阀	jūnfá	warlord

163

折磨	折磨	zhémó	torment
命運	命运	mìngyùn	fate
播弄		bōnòng	to order somebody about
猶豫	犹豫	yóuyù	hesitation; indecision
衝突	冲突	chōngtū	conflict
義務	义务	yìwù	obligation
擔子	担子	dànzi	burden, load
心目		xīnmù	mind, mental view
固定		gùdìng	fixed
階級	阶级	jiējí	(social) class
成見	成见	chéngjiàn	preconceived idea; prejudice
使命		shǐmìng	mission
真善美		zhēn shàn měi	truth, good and beauty
傷感	伤感	shānggǎn	sentimental
淺薄	浅薄	qiǎnbó	shallow, superficial
人道主義	人道主义	réndàozhǔyì	humanitarianism
無限	无限	wúxiàn	limitless, immeasurable

大聲疾呼	大声疾呼	dà shēng jí hū	loudly appeal to the public
水深火熱	水深火热	shuǐ shēn huǒ rè	deep water and scorching fire- an abyss of suffering
視若無睹	视若无睹	shì ruò wú dǔ	to take no notice of what one sees
鼻涕		bítì	nasal mucus
訴苦	诉苦	sùkǔ	to vent one's grievances
申冤	申冤	shēnyuān	to redress an injustice
吟風弄月	吟风弄月	yín fēng nòng yuè	to sing of the moon and the wind- sentimental verse
情詩	情诗	qíngshī	love poem
貴族	贵族	guìzú	noble, aristocrat
資產階級	资产阶级	zīchǎnjiējí	bourgeois class
罪名		zuìmíng	accusation
矛盾		máodùn	contradiction
描寫	描写	miáoxiě	to describe
到頭來	到头来	dàotóulái	in the end, finally
表現	表现	biǎoxiàn	manifestation
帝國主義	帝国主义	dìguózhǔyì	imperialism
反映		fǎnyìng	reflection

失戀	失恋	shīliàn	to be disappointed in love
春花秋月		chūn huā qiū yuè	spring flower and autumn moon--the best things at the best times
感慨		gǎnkǎi	emotional excitement
忠於	忠于	zhōngyú	to be loyal to
修養	修养	xiūyǎng	accomplishment, training
材料		cáiliào	material
浪漫運動	浪漫运动	làngmàn yùndòng	romanticism, a literary, artistic, and philosophical movement originating in the 18th century, characterized chiefly by a reaction against neoclassicism and an emphasis on the imagination and emotions
個性	个性	gèxìng	personality
趨向	趋向	qūxiàng	trend, direction
解放		jiěfàng	liberation
密切		mìqiè	close, intimate
禮教	礼教	lǐjiào	the Confucian ethical code
條規	条规	tiáoguī	rules and regulations
壓抑	压抑	yāyì	suppression, oppression
倡導	倡导	chàngdǎo	to initiate; initiation
比擬	比拟	bǐnǐ	comparison, metaphor

遵奉		zūnfèng	to revere, to venerate
崇拜		chóngbài	to worship
無產階級	无产阶级	wúchǎnjiējí	the proletarian class
氣息	气息	qìxī	flavor
平民		píngmín	the common people
屬於	属于	shǔyú	to belong to
珍寶	珍宝	zhēnbǎo	treasure
欣賞	欣赏	xīnshǎng	to appreciate; to enjoy
批判		pīpàn	to criticize
品味		pǐnwèi	a taste/feel for art
鑒賞	鉴赏	jiànshǎng	to appreciate (art)
貧賤	贫贱	pínjiàn	poor and lowly
富貴	富贵	fùguì	wealth and rank
界限		jièxiàn	dividing line
疑心		yíxīn	to suspect
歌謠	歌谣	gēyáo	ballad, folk song
聚於一堂	聚于一堂	yùyúyītáng	to gather together

你一言我一語		nǐ yī yán wǒ yī yǔ	one word from you and one word from me--with everybody joining in
你一言我一语			
附和		fùhè	to echo, to chime with
吶喊		nàhǎn	to shout loudly, to cry out
原始		yuánshǐ	primitive
願望	愿望	yuànwàng	desire, wish
牧師	牧师	mùshī	minister
傳教	传教	chuánjiào	to proselytize
武器		wǔqì	weapon
手段		shǒuduàn	means, measure
熱情	热情	rèqíng	passion
滲入	渗入	shènrù	to infiltrate
無意	无意	wúyì	accidentally; unintentionally
感人		gǎnrén	moving, touching
終結	终结	zhōngjié	to end
效用		xiàoyòng	effectiveness, usefulness
截止		jiézhǐ	to end, to close
不啻		búchì	to be equivalent to, to be exactly like

譏諷	讥讽	jīfěng	to ridicule
嘲弄		cháonòng	to mock
平心靜氣	平心静气	píngxīnjìngqì	calmly, dispassionately
發揚	发扬	fāyáng	to develop, to carry forward
鼓吹		gǔchuī	to advocate, to uphold

文学与革命
词语例句

一. （对...）加以　　　（used to formalize the following verb.）

※ 文学与革命之间的关系是我们平常不大注意的一个问题，而又是我们不能不加以考虑的。

1. 在今天的演讲里，我想对环境污染的问题加以讨论。

2. 研究政治问题时，我们必须对经济也加以注意。

二. S.之所以...，（不过）是因为...　　　the reason that

※ 天才之所以成为天才，不过是因为他的天赋特别厚些，眼光特别强些。

1. 台湾的自然条件并不好，它的经济之所以发达，不过是因为经济政策的正确。

2. 他既不用功，又不聪明，他成绩之所以不错，不过是因为运气好。

三. 偏偏　　　（contrary to what is expected）

※ 一般民众所不能感觉、所不能透视、所不能领悟的，天才偏偏能。

1. 他父母不要他做的事，他偏偏去做。

2. 他是一个怪人。别人所不喜欢的，他偏偏喜欢。

四. 无论　　　no matter what, how, etc.

※ 无论是政治的组织或是社会的结合，总是比较优秀的份子占领袖或统治者的地位。

1. 无论做什么都解决不了这个问题。

2. 无论在哪一个时代，人民对政府的基本要求都是一样的。

五. 以　　　in order to, so as to

※ 比较优秀的分子，如完全是依赖他的聪明才智以达到这种地位，

这便是一个常态的路程。

1．没想到他居然用这种不合法的手段以达到他的目的。

2．我们必须牺牲个人以符合社会的利益。

六．在于　　　　　　　　　　　　　　　　　　　to lie in

※ 少数的优秀的天才的任务，即在于根据他的才智为团体谋最大的幸福。

1．中国最大的问题即在于人口太多。

2．父母与子女的代沟即在于教育所造成的思想差距。

七．进而　　　　　　　　　　to proceed to（the next step）

※ 革命的意义既如上述，请进而讨论革命与文学的关系。

1．既然大家已同意"道德"这个词的意义，我们就可以进而讨论什么是"道德堕落"。

2．我们得先明白"民主"的意义，才能进而研究民主在中国实行的可能性。

八．何以　　　　　　　　　　　　　　　　　　　　　why

※ 我们并不能说，在革命时期，一切的作家必须创作革命的文学。何以呢?

1．何以在五十年代为世界第一富国的美国，三十年后会衰落呢?

2．何以追求民主自由的五四运动过去七十年之后，中国的大学生还在争取民主呢?

九．与其 A，毋宁 B　　　　　better be B rather than A

※ 与其说先有革命后有革命的文学，毋宁说先有革命的文学后有革命。

1．与其失去自由，毋宁失去生命。因为没有自由的生命毫无意义。

2．与其整日空想，毋宁多作实验。

十. 站在....的立场上　　　　　　　　　　　to be at the stand point of

※ 站在实际的革命者的立场上来观察，我们可以说这是"革命的文学"，那是"不革命的文学"。

1. 站在中国的立场上，中日战争是日本军阀侵略中国。站在日本军阀的立场上，他们却说日本进入中国。

2. 站在教育工作者的立场，我不能因为这个孩子的家庭贫穷就不好好的教导他。

十一. 难道...吗?　　　　　　　　　　Do you really mean to say that

※ 难道生老病死的折磨不是痛苦?难道命运的播弄不是痛苦?

1. 你已经作了父亲，难道你还不了解父亲对孩子的爱?

2. 难道你成年以后结了婚，还要住在父母家里?

十二. 到头来　　　　　　　　　　　　　　in the end, finally

※ 一个文人无论描写什么，到头来还不是个人心理的表现?

1. 你如果不建立自己的公司，只是替别人工作，那么你工作了一辈子，到头来还不是什么都没有?

2. 由于他的理论错误，虽然他研究了很长的时间，到头来什么成绩都没有。

十三. 在...（的眼里）看来　　　　　　　to view from the point of

※ 在革命家的眼里看来，个人主义的文学恐怕不能算是革命的。

1. 在老师的眼里看来，用功的学生才是好学生。

2. 在共产主义者眼里看来，比别人富有是一种罪恶。

十四. 就...而言　　　　　　　　　　　　as far as ... is concerned

※ 就文学作品与读者的关系而言，我们看不见阶级的界限。

1. 就女权运动而言，六十年代是最积极的时代。

2. 就中文而言，这学期大家的进步都很大。

十五. 不啻　　　　　　　　　　　　　　to be exactly like

※ 把文学的性质限于"革命的"，不啻把文学的价值降低。

1. 反对共产党的领导，不啻反对中国政府的政策。

2. 把"右派"的罪名加在他身上，不啻判了他的死刑。

（十二）

自由與平等

平等		píngděng	equality
法蘭西	法兰西	Fǎlánxī	法國
沿用		yányòng	to continue to use old methods (an old system)
爭論	争论	zhēnglùn	dispute; controversy
含義	含义	hányì	implication, connotation
考驗	考验	kǎoyàn	test; trial
形態	形态	xíngtài	form
費	费	fèi	to require a lot of
解釋	解释	jiěshì	to explain
口號	口号	kǒuhào	slogan
經不起	经不起	jīngbùqǐ	to fail to stand or pass (a test or trial)
幻想		huànxiǎng	fantasy
表面		biǎomiàn	on the surface
恢復	恢复	huīfù	to restore, to revive
中古		zhōnggǔ	medieval times

階級	阶级	jiējí	(social) class
政權	政权	zhèngquán	political power; regime
中葉	中叶	zhōngyè	中期
馬克思	马克思	Mǎkèsī	Karl Marx (1818-1883)
呼聲	呼声	hūshēng	call
包括		bāokuò	including
無政府主義	无政府主义	wúzhèngfǔzhǔyì	anarchism
無産階級	无产阶级	wúchǎnjiējí	the proletariat
專政	专政	zhuānzhèng	dictatorship
抹煞		mǒshā	to erase; to blot out
蘇聯	苏联	Sūlián	the Soviet Union
號召	号召	hàozhào	appeal; call
欺騙	欺骗	qīpiàn	trickery; deceit
瞞不了		mánbùliǎo	骗不了
形態	形态	xíngtài	form
斯大林		Sīdàlín	Joseph V. Stalin (1879-1953)
別派		biépài	another faction

墨索里尼		Mòsuǒlǐní	Benito Mussolini (1883-1945)
列寧	列宁	Lièníng	Nikolai Lenin (1870-1924)
背叛		bèipàn	to betray
極端	极端	jíduān	extremely
惋惜		wǎnxī	覺得可惜
若干		ruògān	一些；好幾
提倡		tíchàng	to advocate
特殊		tèshū	特別
權能	权能	quánnéng	權力和作用
寡頭	寡头	guǎtóu	oligarch
乃是		nǎishì	是
吃不消		chībuxiāo	受不了
終究	终究	zhōngjiū	到底，after all
巧妙		qiǎomiào	clever
程序		chéngxù	procedure
培養	培养	péiyǎng	to foster; to develop
施政		shīzhèng	administrative

作風	作风	zuòfēng	style of doing things
訓典	训典	xùndiǎn	instructional quotation
荒誕不經	荒诞不经	huāngdànbùjīng	preposterous; absurd
烏托邦主義	乌托邦主义	Wūtuōbāngzhǔyì	Utopianism
虛僞	虚伪	xūwěi	hypocritical
極度	极度	jídù	to the utmost
特務	特务	tèwù	spy; secret agent
妨礙	妨碍	fáng'ài	to obstruct
何嘗	何尝	hécháng	用於反問：哪裡，怎麼，並不
俄國	俄国	Ēguó	Russia
非		fēi	不是
政治局		zhèngzhìjú	the Political Bureau
委員	委员	wěiyuán	member
普通		pǔtōng	ordinary
要..的命		yào...demìng	要...去死
糾正	纠正	jiūzhèng	to correct
誠然	诚然	chéngrán	的確

憲法	宪法	xiànfǎ	constitution
天花亂墜	天花乱坠	tiān huā luàn zhuì	to give an extravagantly colorful description
大意		dàyì	general idea
醒覺者	醒觉者	xǐngjuézhě	awakener
蘇維埃	苏维埃	Sūwéi'aī	Soviet
意識	意识	yìshí	ideology
聯邦	联邦	liánbāng	union
共和國	共和国	gònghéguó	republic
乾脆	干脆	gāncuì	simply
主權	主权	zhǔquán	sovereign rights
廢話	废话	fèihuà	nonsense
贊成	赞成	zànchéng	to favor
因而		yīnér	所以
仔細	仔细	zǐxì	careful
不然		bùrán	不是那麼回事
狀態	状态	zhuàngtài	state; condition
固然		gùrán	no doubt that

相當	相当	xiāngdāng	very much; quite
特權	特权	tèquán	privilege
支配		zhīpèi	to control
漠視	漠视	mòshì	to ignore; to pay no attention to
無限	无限	wúxiàn	limitless
發揮	发挥	fāhuī	to bring into play
舉（例）	举（例）	jǔ (lì)	to cite or give example
實例	实例	shílì	real example
資本家	资本家	zīběnjiā	capitalists
杜魯門	杜鲁门	Dùlǔmén	Harry S. Truman (1884-1972)
無可奈何	无可奈何	wú kě nài hé	一點辦法也沒有
前進	前进	qiánjìn	advanced
假如		jiǎrú	如果
華萊士	华莱士	Huáláishì	personal name
北冰洋		Běibīngyáng	the Arctic Ocean
財富	财富	cáifù	wealth
分配		fēnpèi	to distribute

平均		píngjūn	to share equally
集中		jízhōng	to centralize
豈不	岂不	qǐbú	wouldn't that...?
深切		shēnqiè	deeply
充分		chōngfèn	fully
極權	极权	jíquán	extremely centralized power
危害		wēihài	harm
波羅底海	波罗底海	Bōluódǐhǎi	the Baltic (Sea)
黑海		Hēihǎi	the Black Sea
岸		àn	coast
土耳其		Tǔěrqí	Turkey
猶太人	犹太人	Yóutàirén	Jew
僅次於	仅次于	jǐncìyú	second only to
希特勒		Xītèlē	Adolf Hitler (1889-1945) (Nazi Party leader from Germany)
人道主義	人道主义	réndàozhǔyì	humanitarianism
儘管	尽管	jǐnguǎn	in spite; even though; no matter if
殘酷	残酷	cánkù	cruel

禍根	祸根	huògēn	bane; cause of ruin
種	种	zhòng	to plant
奇形怪狀	奇形怪状	qíxíng guàizhuàng	grotesque shape and appearance
公敵	公敌	gōngdí	public enemy
然而		rán'ér	可是
打動	打动	dǎdòng	使人感動
所謂	所谓	suǒwèi	so-called
心坎		xīnkǎn	the bottom of one's heart
闊綽	阔绰	kuòchuò	extravagant
換取		huànqǔ	to exchange
統治階級	统治阶级	tǒngzhìjiējí	ruling clan
何須乎	何须乎	héxūhū	何必要
過程	过程	guòchéng	process
結論	结论	jiélùn	conclusion
有心		yǒuxīn	故意
難解	难解	nánjiě	hard to explain
失敗	失败	shībài	failure

虛僞	虛伪	xūwěi	dishonest, hypocritical
有過之而無不及 有过之而无不及		yǒu guò zhī ér wú bù jí	to go even further than; to outdo (bad connotation)
與其A毋寧B 与其A毋宁B		yǔqí...wúnìng...	A is not as good as B
保持		bǎochí	to maintain; to preserve
暫時	暂时	zànshí	temporarily
放棄	放弃	fàngqì	to give up
奮鬥	奋斗	fèndòu	to struggle
餘地	余地	yúdì	leeway; room

自由与平等

词语例句

一. 固然... , 但...   it is true that ..., but

※ "自由"固然有很多不同的形态,但"平等"二字比自由还费解
释。

1. 妇女的权力固然已有增加,但离理想的情况还差很远。

2. 在传统社会中,女孩子固然没有受教育的权利,男孩子所受的教育
也很有限。

二. 表面上... , 事实上...   on the surface ... ,but in fact

※ 苏联的制度,表面(上)说是经济平等,事实上恢复了中古的阶
级政权形式的不平等。

1. 表面上中美关系十分友好,事实上双方经常互相批评。

2. 中国的经济在表面上快速发展,事实上有许多问题需要解决。

三. 包括...在内   including

※ 一切的社会主义者都是用自由这个呼声的,包括无政府主义在内。

1. 所有学习外语的人包括中文老师在内都承认学习中文需要较长的
时间。

2. 全校的人数,包括教职员在内,一共有六千多人。

四. 极端 adj.   to be extremely adj.

※ 他背叛共党的时候,列宁是极端惋惜的。

1. 学外语对老年人来说是极端困难的。

2. 对这种极端激进的理论,我们得特别小心。

五. ...之至   to be adj. to the utmost

※ 这真是荒诞不经之至了。

　　1．想用这么简单的方法治理一个土地面积如此广大的国家，完全是荒唐之至。

　　2．你以为你的非法行为不会被发现? 你真是糊涂之至。

六．一向　　　　　　　　　　　　　　　　always, all along

　　※ 马克思一向批评别派的社会主义是乌托邦主义者。

　　1．中国一向是一个以农业为主的社会。

　　2．联合国一向以维持世界和平为宗旨。

七．何尝　　　　　　（rhetorical question）how could it be that

　　※ 过分的组织固然妨碍"自由"，过分的组织又何尝不妨碍"平等"?

　　1．学生固然喜欢放假，老师何尝不喜欢放假?

　　2．你说你没有经验，我又何尝有经验呢?

八．给...留余地　　　　　　　　　　　to leave some margin for

　　※ 政权如此集中，绝不给私人留点余地，岂不更影响自由?

　　1．你不要逼他逼得太紧，最好给他留一点余地，要不然他会恨你的。

　　2．要革命，就必须作彻底的改革，不能给残留的坏传统留一点余地。

九．岂不　　　　　　　　　　　　　　　　Wouldn't it...

　　※ 政权如此集中，绝不给私人留点余地，岂不更影响自由?

　　1．这么长的报告，用电脑来写岂不是快得多?

　　2．苏联的灭亡岂不正说明社会主义有问题?

十．尽管　　　　　　　　　　　　　　although, even though

　　※ 苏联在列宁时代，还多少有人道主义，尽管残酷的祸根已种在那个时候。

　　1．他还是要试行这个办法，尽管他已料到会有许多困难。

　　2．尽管社会问题不少，美国还是许多人向往的国家。

十一. 与其A,毋宁B　　　　　　　　　Better be B rather than A

※ 与其要求绝对的平等而受骗，毋宁保持着相当大量的自由而暂时放弃一部分的经济平等。

1. 与其用一个聪明而工作不努力的人，毋宁用一个努力而不那么聪明的人。

2. 与其为了个人自由而使国家灭亡，毋宁暂时牺牲个人自由而保全国家。

十二. 有...的余地　　　　　　　　　there is still room for

※ 这样，将来还有奋斗的余地。

1. 这件事已经决定了，没有商量的余地。

2. 在全体会员投票通过以前，还有改变的余地。

(十三)

中國與日本

培利		Péilì	Admiral Perry
上將	上将	shàngjiàng	admiral (in navy)
抵達	抵达	dǐdá	到達
單純	单纯	dānchún	simple and pure
海軍	海军	hǎijūn	navy
混合體	混合体	hùnhétǐ	mixture
來源	来源	láiyuán	origin
分支		fēnzhī	part; branch
主體	主体	zhǔtǐ	main body
相似		xiāngsì	差不多
遽下斷語	遽下断语	jù xià duànyǔ	to jump to conclusions
差以毫釐	差以毫厘	chāyǐháolí	(由於)非常小的差別
謬以千里	谬以千里	miùyǐqiānlǐ	(結果)造成很大的錯誤
變質	变质	biànzhì	to deteriorate
支流		zhīliú	tributary

186

導源於	导源于	dǎoyuányú	to originate from
可貴	可贵	kěguì	valuable
成份		chéngfèn	elements
西域		xīyù	the Western Regions (a Han Dynasty term for the area west of Yumenguan including Xinjiang and parts of Central Asia)
印度		Yìndù	India
伊斯蘭	伊斯兰	Yīsīlán	Islam
希臘	希腊	Xīlà	Greece
歷經	历经	lìjīng	to undergo; to experience
異族	异族	yìzú	different race or nation
逐漸	逐渐	zhújiàn	gradually
衰落		shuāiluò	to decline; to deteriorate
尚武		shàngwǔ	to be militaristic
吸收		xīshōu	to absorb
佛教		Fójiào	Buddhism
南宋		NánSòng	the Southern Song Dynasty (1127-1279)
鎌倉	镰仓	Liáncāng	the Kamakura Era in Japan's history (1192-1333)

朱子		Zhūzǐ	朱熹(南宋哲學家, 1130 - 1200)
明末		Míngmò	the last period of the Ming Dynasty
德川氏		Déchuānshì	the Tokugawa Shogunate (1603-1867)
本		běn	根據
禪僧	禅僧	chánsēng	Buddhist monk
夙志		sùzhì	long-cherished wish
廣招	广招	guāngzhāo	to recruit, enlist, invite from a wide range
刻書	刻书	kèshū	to engrave books
極一時之盛	极一时之盛	jí yì shí zhī shèng	to enjoy great popularity
威力		wēilì	power
興國	兴国	xīngguó	for a nation to flourish
張本	张本	zhāngběn	foundation; corner-stone
道德		dàodé	morality
民間	民间	mínjiān	老百姓中間
咸(豐)	咸(丰)	Xiánfēng	the title of an emperor's reign during the Qing Dynasty (1851-1861)
同(治)	同(治)	Tóngzhì	the title of an emperor's reign during the Qing Dynasty (1862-1874)
明治維新	明治维新	Míngzhìwéixīn	Japan's Meiji period (1868-1912)

經世	经世	jīngshì	治國 (to govern/administer a nation)
相接引		xiāngjiēyǐn	to combine, to integrate
遂		suì	因此；thereupon
史無前例	史无前例	shǐ wú qián lì	unprecedented
致		zhì	使...到了（變成）...
境		jìng	condition; situation
予		yǔ	給
鼓勵	鼓励	gǔlì	encouragement
興奮	兴奋	xīngfèn	excitement
幼年		yòunián	childhood
奉...爲	奉...为	fèng...wéi	to look up to ... as to esteem ... as
反哺		fǎnbǔ	to repay (to return a favor)
復興	复兴	fùxīng	to revive; to be rejuvenated
秉國	秉国	bǐngguó	to dominate a country
軍閥	军阀	jūnfá	warlord
盡忠	尽忠	jìnzhōng	to express/show loyalty
施恕		shīshù	to grant forgiveness

義	义	yì	justice and virtue
仁		rén	charity; mercy; kindness; benevolence
致使		zhìshǐ	使
慘痛	惨痛	cǎntòng	painful
終致	终致	zhōngzhì	at long last leading to
鷸蚌相爭漁翁得利 鷸蚌相争渔翁得利		yù bàng xiāng zhēng yú wēng dé lì	When the snipe and the clam are locked in combat, it's the fisherman who benefits. It's the third party that benefits from the struggle
幕		mù	an act of a play
悲劇	悲剧	bēijù	tragedy
此後	此后	cǐhòu	以後
大陸	大陆	dàlù	mainland
越南		Yuènán	Vietnam
亦		yì	也
猶	犹	yóu	像；如
若		ruò	如果
抱		bào	to hold (an idea)
狹義	狭义	xiáyì	narrow sense

實際言之	实际言之	shíjì yán zhī	as a matter of fact
包含		bāohán	to contain; to include
因素		yīnsù	factor
其來甚漸	其来甚渐	qí lái shèn jiàn	its coming was gradual
故不自覺耳	故不自觉耳	gù bú zì jué ěr	it's only that one doesn't feel it
不知不覺	不知不觉	bù zhī bù jué	unwittingly; unawares
大幸		dàxìng	great good fortune
也		yě	sentence ending particle meaning 是
善於	善于	shànyú	to be good at; to be adept in
效法		xiàofǎ	to emulate after
立國	立国	lìguó	to establish a country
訓練	训练	xùnliàn	to train
陸軍	陆军	lùjūn	the army
殖民帝國	殖民帝国	zhímíndìguó	colonial empire
閃電	闪电	shǎndiàn	lightning
戰術	战术	zhànshù	military tactics
發動	发动	fādòng	to launch

珍珠港		Zhēnzhūgǎng	Pearl Harbor
突襲	突袭	tūxí	surprise attack
欽佩	钦佩	qīnpèi	to admire
模仿		mófǎng	to imitate
彌補	弥补	míbǔ	to make up; to remedy
缺憾		quēhàn	weakness; defect
衰亡		shuāiwáng	to decline and fall
饑饉	饥馑	jījǐn	famine
災禍	灾祸	zāihuò	disaster
精疲力竭		jīng pí lì jié	exhausted; drained
種籽	种籽	zhǒngzǐ	seeds
俱		jù	全，都，一塊儿
矛盾		máodùn	contradictory
溶而爲一	溶而为一	róng ér wéi yī	to fuse into one
空前		kōngqián	unprecedented
歸功於	归功于	guīgōngyú	to give credit to
依循		yīxún	to follow

路線	路线	lùxiàn	route
世襲	世袭	shìxí	hereditary
統治階級	统治阶级	tǒngzhìjiējí	the ruling class
孕育於	孕育于	yùnyùyú	to be bred or nurtured in
領袖	领袖	lǐngxiù	leader
精忠不二		jīng zhōng bú èr	absolutely loyal
美德		měidé	virtue
擁護	拥护	yōnghù	to support (a leader)
服從	服从	fúcóng	to obey
堅定不移	坚定不移	jiān dìng bù yí	firm and unswerving
朝着		cháozhe	toward
固定		gùdìng	fixed
基層	基层	jīcéng	primary level; basic level
由下而上		yóu xià ér shàng	從下到上
相當於	相当于	xiāngdāngyú	to be about equal to; more or less
士大夫		shìdàfu	literati and officialdom (in feudal China)
遼闊	辽阔	liáokuò	vast and extensive

國度	国度	guódù	國家
萬眾一心	万众一心	wàn zhòng yì xīn	millions of people all of one mind
仰仗		yǎngzhàng	to look up to someone for support; to rely on
驅策	驱策	qūcè	to steer and drive
督導	督导	dūdǎo	to supervise and direct
過程	过程	guòchéng	process
緩慢	缓慢	huǎnmàn	慢
迂迴曲折	迂回曲折	yū huí qū zhé	full of twists and turns; circuitous
孫中山	孙中山	Sūn Zhōngshān	Sun Yat-sen (1868 - 1940)
章太炎		Zhāng Tàiyán	章炳麟，學者；民主革命家 (1869-1936)
梁任公		Liáng Rèngōng	梁啓超，學者 (1873-1929)
蔡孑民		Cài Jiémín	蔡元培，學者，教育家 (1868-1940)
諸	诸	zhū	各位
遠見	远见	yuǎnjiàn	foresight, far-seeing; wisdom
深入		shēnrù	to immerse oneself in
係	系	xì	to be
平民		píngmín	the common people

締造	缔造	dìzào	to create
任意		rènyì	at will
獨裁	独裁	dúcái	to rule autocratically
具備	具备	jùbèi	to possess; to have
超人		chāorén	to be above average, outstanding
才智		cáizhì	wisdom and ability
採取	采取	cǎiqǔ	to adopt
措施		cuòshī	measures
每		měi	often
遲緩	迟缓	chíhuǎn	slow
一旦		yīdàn	once; as soon as
徹底	彻底	chèdǐ	thoroughly, completely
炮彈	炮弹	pàodàn	artillery shell
着手		zhuóshǒu	開始
進而	进而	jìnér	then; to proceed to the next step
從事	从事	cóngshì	to take up a matter
乃至		nǎizhì	一直到...; and even

195

揚棄	扬弃	yángqì	to discard
信仰		xìnyǎng	conviction; belief
另行		lìngxíng	另外
輕易	轻易	qīngyì	easily; carelessly
同化		tónghuà	to assimilate
納	纳	nà	to adopt; to incorporate
仍舊	仍旧	réngjiù	仍然
落		luò	to fall; to lag behind
兼		jiān	and; concurrently
天性使然		tiānxìng shǐ rán	nature makes it so; natural tendency
胸襟寬大	胸襟宽大	xiōngjīn kuāndà	open-minded
自立		zìlì	independently
組織	组织	zǔzhī	organization
紀律	纪律	jìlǜ	discipline
優點	优点	yōudiǎn	strong point
弱點	弱点	ruòdiǎn	weak point
優劣互見	优劣互见	yōu liè hù jiàn	to have both virtues and defects

鬥士	斗士	dòushì	warrior
幹練	干练	gànliàn	capable and experienced
行政人員	行政人员	xíngzhèng rényuán	administrator
上層結構	上层结构	shàngcéngjiégòu	superstructure
觸及	触及	chùjí	to touch upon; to reach
中世紀	中世纪	zhōngshìjì	Middle Ages
驚奇	惊奇	jīngqí	to be surprised
封建制度		fēngjiànzhìdù	feudal system
廢除	废除	fèichú	to abolish; to abrogate
甚		shèn	非常
西曆	西历	xīlì	公曆
紀元	纪元	jìyuán	公元
忠		zhōng	loyalty
恕		shù	forgiveness
然而		ránér	可是
恕道		shùdào	the way to forgive
指導	指导	zhǐdǎo	guidance

原則	原則	yuánzé	principle
黷武	黩武	dúwǔ	militaristic; bellicose
必不可少		bì bù kě shǎo	必須有
品德		pǐndé	moral quality
堅執己見	坚执己见	jiān zhí jǐ jiàn	persistent in one's own opinions
胸襟狹窄	胸襟狭窄	xiōngjīn xiázhǎi	narrow-minded
偏狹	偏狭	piānxiá	apt to be narrow and limited
心理		xīnlǐ	mentality
洲際	洲际	zhōujì	intercontinental
野心		yěxīn	ambition
武力		wǔlì	military force
風度	风度	fēngdù	demeanor; bearing
携手同行		xié shǒu tóng xíng	to go hand in hand
忠貞	忠贞	zhōngzhēn	to be loyal and steadfast
設想	设想	shèxiǎng	to give thought to; to take into consideration
忠於	忠于	zhōngyú	to be loyal to
排斥		páichì	to exclude

設身處地	设身处地	shè shēn chǔ dì	to put oneself in someone else's position
所謂	所谓	suǒwèi	that which is called
薄弱		bóruò	weak
行爲	行为	xíngwéi	deeds; behavior
健壯	健壮	jiànzhuàng	robust
頑童	顽童	wántóng	naughty kid
抓住		zhuāzhù	to hold on to
公羊		gōngyáng	ram
角		jiǎo	horn
撞		zhuàng	to hit; to strike; to butt
反應	反应	fǎnyìng	reaction
好戰	好战	hàozhàn	bellicose; warlike
信念		xìnniàn	belief
神聖	神圣	shénshèng	holy; sacred
神		shén	a god
意志		yìzhì	will
行事		xíngshì	to act

征服		zhēngfú	to conquer
軍閥	军阀	jūnfá	warlord
御用		yùyòng	to utilize; to use
歪曲		wāiqū	to distort
史實	史实	shǐshí	historical facts
深信不疑		shēnxìnbùyí	to believe without the slightest doubt
神佛		shénfó	Gods and Buddhas
監護者	监护者	jiānhùzhě	guardian
呵護者	呵护者	hēhùzhě	protector
稱霸	称霸	chēngbà	to achieve hegemony; to dominate
意旨		yìzhǐ	wish; will
宗教		zōngjiào	religion
狂熱	狂热	kuángrè	fanaticism
削弱		xuēruò	to weaken
解體	解体	jiětǐ	to disintegrate
團結一致	团结一致	tuánjié yízhì	to unite as one
強烈		qiángliè	intense; strong

形成		xíngchéng	to form
無理可喻	无理可喻	wú lǐ kě yù	can't be reasoned with; unreasonable
制服		zhìfú	to bring under control
威脅	威胁	wēixié	menace; threat
瘋狂	疯狂	fēngkuáng	crazy
動亂	动乱	dòngluàn	turmoil
豈	岂	qǐ	哪裡
僅	仅	jǐn	只是
國策	国策	guócè	national policy
軍國主義	军国主义	jūnguózhǔyì	militarism
財富	财富	cáifù	wealth
財閥	财阀	cáifá	financial magnate; tycoon
聯合	联合	liánhé	to unite
操縱	操纵	cāozòng	to exercise (power)
軍政大權	军政大权	jūnzhèngdàquán	military and government power
超越		chāoyuè	to go beyond; to exceed
黨派	党派	dǎngpài	political parties

學派	学派	xuépài	school of thought
橫衝直撞	横冲直撞	héng chōng zhí zhuàng	to dash around madly
轟炸	轰炸	hōngzhà	to bomb
內政		nèizhèng	internal affairs
倒幕尊皇		dǎo mù zūn huáng	to rebel against shogunate government and respect the imperial family
保皇		bǎohuáng	royalist
繼	继	jì	後來
軍閥割據	军阀割据	jūnfágējù	separatist warlord regimes
擾攘	扰攘	rǎorǎng	turmoil
國民革命軍	国民革命军	guómín gémìngjūn	the National Revolutionary Army
稱兵	称兵	chēngbīng	to set up a military force
內憂外患	内忧外患	nèi yōu wài huàn	domestic trouble and foreign invasions
接踵而起		jiē zhǒng ér qǐ	to happen successively; one after another
儒家		Rújiā	Confucianist
不患寡而患不均		bú huàn guǎ ér huàn bù jūn	to consider inequality but not scarcity to be a problem
先天		xiāntiān	innately
贊成	赞成	zànchéng	to favor, to approve

否定		fǒudìng	to deny; to negate
以此而論	以此而论	yǐ cǐ ér lùn	to talk about this
門戶開放	门户开放	ménhù kāifàng	open door
均		jūn	都
鎖國主義	锁国主义	suǒguózhǔyì	closed-door policy
稱之爲	称之为	chēngzhīwéi	to call it...
通商		tōngshāng	having trade relations
然		rán	不過
發之於	发之于	fāzhīyú	由...開始的
實效	实效	shíxiào	actual effect
此開彼閉	此开彼闭	cǐ kāi bǐ bì	as one opens, another closes
前迎後拒	前迎后拒	qián yíng hòu jù	to greet (welcome) first and then reject
步驟	步骤	bùzhòu	steps, procedure
顯	显	xiǎn	noticeable
瓜分		guāfēn	to carve up
禍兆	祸兆	huòzhào	an evil omen
抗戰	抗战	Kàngzhàn	Anti-Japanese War (1937-1945)

重慶	重庆	Chóngqìng	city in Sichuan province
蹂躪	蹂躏	róulìn	to trample upon
鐵蹄	铁蹄	tiětí	iron heel (cruel oppressions of the people)
犧牲	牺牲	xīshēng	to sacrifice
客觀	客观	kèguān	to be objective
公平		gōngpíng	fair
平衡		pínghéng	balance
和約	和约	héyuē	peace treaty
維持	维持	wéichí	to maintain; to support
放棄	放弃	fàngqì	to give up
賠款	赔款	péikuǎn	to pay an indemnity; reparations
遣送		qiǎnsòng	to repatriate
全體	全体	quántǐ	entire; all
俘虜	俘虏	fúlǔ	P.O.W.
返國	返国	fǎnguó	to return to one's own country
凡此種種	凡此种种	fán cǐ zhǒng zhǒng	所有這一切
出於	出于	chūyú	to stem from; to be out of ...

不念舊惡	不念旧恶	bú niàn jiù è	to forget past wrongs
和平		hépíng	peace
要道		yàodào	important method
視察	视察	shìchá	to inspect
俘虜營	俘虏营	fúlǔyíng	P.O.W. camp
湘西		Xiāngxī	the western part of Hunan
漢口	汉口	Hànkǒu	town in the city of Wuhan
民衆	民众	mínzhòng	the masses
嘲笑		cháoxiào	to laugh at; to deride
侮辱		wǔrǔ	to humiliate, to insult
舉動	举动	jǔdòng	act; move
度量		dùliàng	tolerance, capacity for forgiveness
寬宏	宽宏	kuānhóng	lenience; magnanimity
戰敗	战败	zhànbài	to lose a war
頗	颇	pō	非常
論	论	lùn	to comment
神道		shéndào	mysticism

迷信		míxìn	superstition
漸趨	渐趋	jiànqū	to gradually become
重史實	重史实	zhòngshǐshí	to lay stress on historical fact
虛偽	虚伪	xūwěi	sham; hypocrisy
學術研究	学术研究	xuéshùyánjiū	academic research
局勢	局势	júshì	political situation

中国与日本
词语例句

一. 除非   unless

※ 除非你能同时了解中国和西方，你就无法了解日本。

1. 除非你真喜欢，你不必买。

2. 除非你认真学习，你不可能学会一种外国语言。

二. 其中   among （them, which, etc.）

※ 唐代文化中许多可贵的成分，其中包括从西域输入的印度文化，
在中国已逐渐衰落。

1. 美国的社会问题很多，其中吸毒问题最严重。

2. 全校有二万多学生，其中百分之十五是少数民族。

三. 予...以...   to give (somebody something)

※ 明治维新在短短数十年里致日本于盛强之境，并予文化祖国的中
国以极大的鼓励与兴奋。

1. 高犯罪率予人们以极大的威胁。

2. 父母予子女以极深的期望。

四. 善于   to be good at

※ 日本善于效法。

1. 他是一个有名的画家，最善于画人物。

2. 文学家善于用文字表达思想和感情。

五. 在于   to lie in

※ 美国的伟大就在于这两种矛盾因素的溶而为一。

1. 中国最大的问题就在于人口太多。

2. 学习外语就在于勤学苦练。

六. 一旦   once that

※ 中国在采取改革措施方面每较迟缓，但是她一旦决心改革，她总希望能够作得比较彻底。

1. 一个国家的经济一旦衰退，很难在短时间内恢复。

2. 他一旦决心作一件事，一定用尽所有的力量去作。

七. 进而   to proceed to

※ 她从制造炮弹着手，进而从事政治改革，社会改革。

1. 中国先控制人口增长，进而进行经济改革。

2. 道德教育应该从家庭开始，进而扩大到社会。

八. 另行 V.   to alter to

※ 她扬弃了旧的信仰，另行建立新的。

1. 他放弃了旧的专业，另行选择。

2. 旧的方案不受欢迎，我只好另行设计新的计划。

九. 岂仅...而已   （rhetorical question）is it merely...?

※ 在过去六十年的动乱时代里，日本又岂仅使我国头痛而已!

1. 中国被日本侵略岂仅是遭受到一点经济损失而已!

2. 年轻人所应该学的岂仅是书本上的知识而已，他们在作人处世方面也应受到极好的训练。

十. A 则...，B 则...   （used to list more than two things）

※ 我国初则保皇革命，国事未定，继则军阀割据，全国扰壤。

※ 国民革命军统一全国的时候，内则共党称兵，外则日本侵略。

1. 如果学生携枪上学，轻则警告，重则开除。

2. 这种事我是不做的，一则于法不合，二则于心不安。

（十四）

杭州、南京、上海、北京

杭州		Hángzhōu	city in Zhejiang province
富		fù	to be imbued with; to be rich in
勝	胜	shèng	grandeur
洋貨	洋货	yánghuò	**外國東西**
集散地		jísàndì	collection and distribution center
歷代	历代	lìdài	past dynasties
帝都		dìdū	capital of an empire
藝術	艺术	yìshù	art
悠閑	悠闲	yōuxián	leisurely and carefree
浙江		Zhèjiāng	province in southeast China
農夫	农夫	nóngfū	farmer
工匠		gōngjiàng	craftsman; artisan
嬉游		xīyóu	**玩**
求學	求学	qiúxué	to pursue one's studies; to attend school
留美		liúměi	**在美國留學**

繼	继	jì	後來
抗戰	抗战	Kàngzhàn	Anti-Japanese War
下游		xiàyóu	downstream of a river
江南		jiāngnán	south of the lower reaches of the Changjiang River
都市		dūshì	大城市，metropolis
氣候	气候	qìhòu	climate
大致		dàzhì	more or less; approximately
季		jì	season
温和		wēnhé	mild; temperate
宜人		yírén	pleasant; agreeable
楊柳	杨柳	yángliǔ	poplar and willow
發芽	发芽	fāyá	to sprout; to bud
採摘	采摘	cǎizhāi	to pick; to pluck
新枝		xīnzhī	newly-grown twig or branch
裝飾	装饰	zhuāngshì	to decorate
門戶	门户	ménhù	門
迎春		yíngchūn	to welcome spring

轉	转	zhuǎn	to turn (change) into
夕陽	夕阳	xīyáng	the setting sun
詩人	诗人	shīrén	poet
靈感	灵感	línggǎn	inspiration
雨季		yǔjì	rainy season
晴雨參半	晴雨参半	qíng yǔ cān bàn	partly-sunny, partly-rainy
土壤		tǔrǎng	soil
肥沃		féiwò	fertile; rich (soil)
農作物	农作物	nóngzuòwù	crop
稻		dào	paddy (rice)
養蠶	养蚕	yǎngcán	raising silkworms
普遍		pǔbiàn	common
蟹		xiè	crab
蚌		bàng	clam, freshwater mussel
鰻	鳗	mán	eel
蔬菜		shūcài	vegetables
遍地皆是		biàndì jiē shì	什麼地方都有

著名		zhùmíng	很有名
揚州	扬州	Yángzhōu	city in Jiangsu province
材料		cáiliào	ingredient; material
流域		liúyù	river valley
金融		jīnróng	financial; banking
繁榮	繁荣	fánróng	prosperity
歸功於	归功于	guīgōngyú	to be credited to
工商		gōngshāng	industrial and commercial
資本	资本	zīběn	capital
結構	结构	jiégòu	structure
基礎	基础	jīchǔ	foundation; base
商人		shāngrén	businessman
資本家	资本家	zīběnjiā	capitalist; businessman
因而		yīnér	as a result; thus
貴族	贵族	guìzú	aristocrat
階級	阶级	jiējí	(social) class
洋人		yángrén	外國人

生活圈子		shēnghuó quānzi	social circles
仍然		réngrán	還是
謎樣的	谜样的	míyàngde	enigmatic; mysterious
富麗	富丽	fùlì	sumptuous, luxurious
幽邃		yōusuì	secluded and tranquil
洋房		yángfáng	外國樣式的房子
恭順	恭顺	gōngshùn	submissive and respectful
僕人	仆人	púrén	servant
伺候		cìhòu	wait upon, look after
有如		yǒurú	好像
王公貴族	王公贵族	wánggōngguìzú	the nobility
剝削	剥削	bōxuē	exploitation
致富		zhìfù	to become rich
揩油		kāiyóu	to get petty advantages at the expense of others; to skim profits
分肥		fēnféi	to share illegal gains
俱樂部	俱乐部	jùlèbù	social club
拒絕	拒绝	jùjué	to reject, to refuse

華人	华人	huárén	中國人
結識	结识	jiéshí	to get to know (people)
自大		zìdà	arrogant; self-important
無知	无知	wúzhī	ignorant
頑固	顽固	wángù	stubborn; obstinate
歧見	歧见	qíjiàn	discriminatory opinion; prejudice
對於	对于	duìyú	對
發明	发明	fāmíng	invention; discovery
創造	创造	chuàngzào	creation
不聞不問	不闻不问	bù wén bú wèn	to show no interest in; to be indifferent to
本國	本国	běnguó	one's home country
發展	发展	fāzhǎn	to develop
思想		sīxiǎng	ideology; thinking
潮流		cháoliú	tendency; direction
一無所知	一无所知	yì wú suǒ zhī	to be totally ignorant of
唯一		wéiyī	only, sole
目標	目标	mùbiāo	goal

地位		dìwèi	position; status
僅次於	仅次于	jǐncìyú	second only to
買辦	买办	mǎibàn	comprador; purchasing agent
洋主子		yángzhǔzi	foreign master
富足		fùzú	rich, affluent
尊敬		zūnjìng	to respect
洋行		yángháng	foreign firm
嘴巴		zuǐbā	mouth
討	讨	tǎo	to beg
同胞		tóngbāo	compatriot
流口水		liúkǒushuǐ	to salivate, to drool (with greed or envy)
不勝	不胜	búshèng	非常
羨慕		xiànmù	to admire
其		qí	its
尾巴		wěibā	tail
煉金術士	炼金术士	liànjīnshùshì	alchemist
點銅成銀	点铜成银	diǎn tóng chéng yín	to turn copper into silver by touching it

215

點銀成金	点银成金	diǎn yín chéng jīn	to turn silver into gold by touching it
討小老婆	讨小老婆	tǎo xiǎolǎopó	to take a concubine
高明		gāomíng	clever
等		děng	AN for classified or graded things/people
購	购	gòu	買
匯錢	汇钱	huìqián	寄錢
田產	田产	tiánchǎn	land and property
置		zhì	買
偶然		ǒurán	occasionally
探親	探亲	tànqīn	to visit family and relatives
自然而然		zìránérrán	naturally
觸動	触动	chùdòng	to stir up; to touch off
靈機	灵机	língjī	sudden inspiration
身經目睹	身经目睹	shēn jīng mù dǔ	to personally experience and see
絕無	绝无	juéwú	完全沒有
誇張	夸张	kuāzhāng	to exaggerate
開明	开明	kāimíng	enlightened

216

熟悉		shúxī	well-aquainted with, familiar
每當	每当	měidāng	whenever
緊蹙雙眉	紧蹙双眉	jǐn cù shuāng méi	to knit one's brows into a frown
嘆息	叹息	tànxī	to sigh
過剩	过剩	guòshèng	surplus; excess
過活	过活	guòhuó	to make a living; to survive
放棄	放弃	fàngqì	to abandon; to give up
耕作		gēngzuò	farming
貧民窟	贫民窟	pínmínkū	slum
居民		jūmín	residents
低賤	低贱	dījiàn	humble; low and degrading
人力車	人力车	rénlìchē	rickshaw
苦力		kǔlì	coolie
江北		jiāngběi	to the north of the lower reaches of the Changjiang River
貧苦	贫苦	pínkǔ	poor, impoverished
縣份	县份	xiànfèn	counties
萬物之靈	万物之灵	wànwù zhī líng	the most conscious or spiritual of all things on earth

動物	动物	dòngwù	animal
奔跑		bēnpǎo	跑
交通工具		jiāotōnggōngjù	transportation facilities
川流不息		chuān liú bù xí	never-ending; in an endless stream
商業	商业	shāngyè	commercial; business
動脈	动脉	dòngmài	artery
保持		bǎochí	to maintain
循環	循环	xúnhuán	to circulate
構成	构成	gòuchéng	to make up; to constitute
租界		zūjiè	foreign concession
心理		xīnlǐ	mentality
崇拜		chóngbài	to worship
權勢	权势	quánshì	power and influence
講究	讲究	jiǎngjiu	to be meticulous about
包括		bāokuò	including
財力	财力	cáilì	wealth
武力		wǔlì	military power

治外法權	治外法权	zhìwàifǎquán	extraterritoriality
功夫		gōngfu	ability; effort
繪畫	绘画	huìhuà	painting
書法	书法	shūfǎ	calligraphy
音樂	音乐	yīnyuè	music
以及		yǐjí	跟，和
庸俗		yōngsú	vulgar and low
通稱	通称	tōngchēng	popularly known as
海派		hǎipài	"Shanghai style" (extravagant)
相對	相对	xiāngduì	opposite
作風	作风	zuòfēng	style; behavior
京派		jīngpài	"Beijing style" (cultivated)
崇尚		chóngshàng	to uphold; to advocate
意義	意义	yìyì	meaning; significance
深刻		shēnkè	deep; profound
力求		lìqiú	努力追求
完美		wánměi	perfection

海洋		hǎiyáng	oceans
沙漠		shāmò	desert
螞蟻	蚂蚁	mǎyǐ	ant
忙忙碌碌		mángmánglùlù	忙
聚斂	聚敛	jùliǎn	to amass (wealth)
敬重		jìngzhòng	to respect
無論	无论	wúlùn	不管（是）
糟糕透頂	糟糕透顶	zāogāotòudǐng	to be in terrible shape
誤解	误解	wùjiě	to misunderstand
文明		wénmíng	civilization
仇恨		chóuhèn	to hate
瞧不起		qiáobuqǐ	看不起
諒解	谅解	liàngjiě	understanding
斂財	敛财	liǎncái	to accumulate wealth by unfair means
因素		yīnsù	factor
終	终	zhōng	終於；最後
難兄難弟	难兄难弟	nán xiōng nán dì	two of a kind; birds of a feather

刮		guā	to extort
揩		kāi	to scrounge; to plunder
綠洲	绿洲	lǜzhōu	oasis
可取之處	可取之处	kě qǔ zhī chù	長處，好處
書籍	书籍	shūjí	書 (collective)
避難所	避难所	bì'nànsuǒ	refuge; asylum
交換		jiāohuàn	to exchange
進化論	进化论	jìnhuàlùn	the Theory of Evolution
種子	种子	zhǒngzǐ	seed
散播		sànbō	to spread, to disseminate
之後	之后	zhīhòu	以後
隨風飄散	随风飘散	suí fēng piāo sàn	to be scattered; to be dispersed
發育	发育	fāyù	to develop
滋長	滋长	zīzhǎng	to grow
合抱大樹	合抱大树	hébàodàshù	a huge tree that one can just get one's arms around
始終	始终	shǐzhōng	從開始到最後
高不盈尺		gāo bù yíng chǐ	不到一尺高

221

民國	民国	mínguó	中華民國
庇護	庇护	bìhù	to protect
軍閥	军阀	jūnfá	warlord
染指		rǎnzhǐ	to encroach on
及		jí	和，跟
掌握		zhǎngwò	to get control of
利用		lìyòng	to use; to take advantage of
管理		guǎnlǐ	management
訣竅	诀窍	juéqiào	knack
宮殿		gōngdiàn	palace
園苑	园苑	yuányuàn	gardens
彼此		bǐcǐ	互相
和睦相處	和睦相处	hémùxiāngchǔ	to get along in harmony
職業	职业	zhíyè	occupation
旗人		qírén	people of the Eight Banners in Qing Dynasty; the Manchu people
平民大衆	平民大众	píngmín dàzhòng	老百姓
融爲一體	融为一体	róng wéi yī tǐ	to fuse into one unit; to be in perfect harmony

生而平等		shēng ér píngděng	to be born equal
出人頭地	出人头地	chū rén tóu dì	to stand out from one's fellows
工程師	工程师	gōngchéngshī	engineer
抽空		chōukòng	擠出時間
欣賞	欣赏	xīnshǎng	to enjoy; to admire
逛		guàng	to go window-shopping
古籍		gǔjí	ancient books
神游		shényóu	to travel in one's imagination; to let one's imagination roam
寶庫	宝库	bǎokù	treasure-house
興致	兴致	xìngzhì	興趣
不妨		bùfáng	可以（作...事）
消磨		xiāomó	to idle/while away (時間)
臨走	临走	línzǒu	快要離開
店夥	店伙	diànhuǒ	shop assistant
再度		zàidù	再次
光臨	光临	guānglín	honor of (your) presence, honor of (your) visit
古董		gǔdǒng	antique; curio

珠寶	珠宝	zhūbǎo	pearls and jewelry
貴重	贵重	guìzhòng	valuable; precious
珍品		zhēnpǐn	treasure
巧妙		qiǎomiào	ingenious
贋品	赝品	yànpǐn	fake; counterfeit; sham
在所不惜		zài suǒ bù xī	will not regret
名伶		mínglíng	famous stage performers
無懈可擊	无懈可击	wú xiè kě jī	flawless; impeccable
動人心弦	动人心弦	dòng rén xīn xián	to tug at one's heart strings
故宮博物院		Gùgōng bówùyuàn	the Palace Museum
歷代	历代	lìdài	past dynasties/ages
天才		tiāncái	genius
創造	创造	chuàngzào	to create
氛圍	氛围	fēnwéi	atmosphere
皇宮		huánggōng	(imperial) palace
內苑		nèiyuàn	(imperial) gardens
青苔		qīngtái	moss

品茗		pǐnmíng	to savor tea
閑眺	闲眺	xiántiào	to leisurely look into the distance
鵝	鹅	é	goose
戲水	戏水	xìshuǐ	玩水
驢	驴	lú	donkey
憑吊	凭吊	píngdiào	to ponder the past while contemplating (a ruin or relic)
名勝古迹	名胜古迹	míngshènggǔjī	scenic spots and historical sites
呼吸		hūxī	to breathe
充塞		chōngsè	充满
古松		gǔsōng	age-old pine trees
芳香		fāngxiāng	fragrant
尋求	寻求	xúnqiú	to seek
正當	正当	zhèngdāng	proper
娛樂	娱乐	yúlè	recreation
一致		yízhì	showing no difference; uniformly
繪圖	绘图	huìtú	畫圖
儀器	仪器	yíqì	apparatus

設計	设计	shèjì	to design
藍圖	蓝图	lántú	blueprint
器皿		qìmǐn	utensils
自然		zìrán	nature
文物		wénwù	cultural relics
獲得	获得	huòdé	to obtain
靈巧	灵巧	língqiǎo	dexterous; skillful
心目		xīnmù	mental view; mind
形象		xíngxiàng	image
戰亂	战乱	zhànluàn	chaos caused by war
易手		yìshǒu	to change hands
國都	国都	guódū	首都
遷移	迁移	qiānyí	搬（到）
仍舊	仍旧	réngjiù	仍然
隨着	随着	suízhe	along with
氣氛	气氛	qìfèn	atmosphere
情趣		qíngqù	quiet appeal to the emotions

血液		xuèyè	血
兩蒙其利	两蒙其利	liǎng méng qí lì	both benefit from it
廢墟	废墟	fèixū	ruins
拆除		chāichú	to tear down; to demolish
新廈		xīnshà	new tall buildings
固然		gùrán	It is true that
憧憬		chōngjǐng	to look forward to
浸淫		jìnyín	to immerse (oneself in)
舊日	旧日	jiùrì	過去
光輝	光辉	guānghuī	glory
記憶	记忆	jìyì	memory
足資依賴	足资依赖	zú zī yīlài	to be enough to rely on
顯得	显得	xiǎndé	to seem; to appear
執行	执行	zhíxíng	to execute, to implement
命令		mìnglìng	an order
悠閑	悠闲	yōuxián	leisurely and unhurried
發榮滋長	发荣滋长	fā róng zī zhǎng	to develop and grow

熙來攘往	熙来攘往	xī lái rǎng wǎng	bustling with activity
爭先恐後	争先恐后	zhēng xiān kǒng hòu	to vie with each other
懶洋洋	懒洋洋	lǎnyángyáng	lazy
感染		gǎnrǎn	to be affected by
加緊	加紧	jiājǐn	to speed up
擁擠	拥挤	yōngjǐ	crowded
角落		jiǎoluò	corner
尚未		shàngwèi	還沒有
栽花		zāihuā	to grow flowers
種木	种木	zhòngmù	to plant trees
焦急		jiāojí	很著急
臨時	临时	línshí	extemporaneous
設法	设法	shèfǎ	想辦法
積極	积极	jījí	enthusiastically; actively
努力不懈		nǔlì búxiè	to make unremitting efforts
辛勤		xīnqín	industrious
終於	终于	zhōngyú	finally

嶄新	崭新	zhǎnxīn	brand-new
繁榮	繁荣	fánróng	prosperous
消失		xiāoshī	to disappear; to vanish
擴散	扩散	kuòsàn	to spread; expand
前途		qiántú	將來（的情形）
大放光明		dàfàng guāngmíng	to shine brightly
或許	或许	huòxǔ	也許
勢必	势必	shìbì	必然，一定
蔭	荫	yìn	shade
鋪築	铺筑	pūzhù	to lay and build (road)
旦夕之間		dànxīzhījiān	早晚之間(表示時間很短)
惶惶不可終日 惶惶不可终日		huáng huáng bù kě zhōng rì	to be on tenterhooks; to be unbearably anxious
流行		liúxíng	popular; fashionable
頗	颇	pō	非常
感慨		gǎnkǎi	feelings and emotions
議而不決	议而不决	yì ér bù jué	討論了而不作決定
決而不辦	决而不办	jué ér bú bàn	決定了而不實行

辦而不通	办而不通	bàn ér bù tōng	實行起來又很難
如此		rúcǐ	這樣；這麼
無可置疑	无可置疑	wú kě zhì yí	毫無疑問；不必問的
相像		xiāngxiàng	相似；像
首府		shǒufǔ	首都 (of a province)
雄偉	雄伟	xióngwěi	grandeur
色調	色调	sèdiào	hue; shade (of colors)
清淡		qīngdàn	mild; light colored
故		gù	所以
個性	个性	gèxìng	individuality, individual character
氣魄	气魄	qìpò	spirit, vigor
究竟		jiūjìng	到底, after all
資產	资产	zīchǎn	property; asset
饒	饶	ráo	to be rich in
文人雅士		wénrén yǎshì	literati and men of letters
風流韻事	风流韵事	fēng liú yùn shì	artsy life-style; Bohemian; romantic affairs
視如拱璧	视如拱璧	shì rú gǒng bì	to treat as if it were precious jade

局限		júxiàn	to be limited
自欺欺人		zì qī qī rén	騙別人也騙自己
太平洋		Tàipíngyáng	the Pacific Ocean
天堂		tiāntáng	paradise
媲美		pìměi	to compare favorably with
俗諺	俗谚	súyàn	common sayings, proverbs
催眠		cuīmián	to mesmerize; to lull to sleep
信以爲真	信以为真	xìn yǐ wéi zhēn	to accept something as true
且		qiě	暫時，暫且, for the time being
證實	证实	zhèngshí	to verify
地震		dìzhèn	earthquake
颱風	台风	táifēng	typhoon
沉醉		chéncuì	to be intoxicated with

杭州、南京、上海、北京
词语例句

一. 归功于   to be credited to

※ 上海的繁荣应该归功于外国人的工商活动。

1. 他的成就要归功于父母不断的鼓励和支持。

2. 台湾的经济繁荣要归功于土地改革的成功。

二. 因而   thus, as a result

※ 外国资本是上海经济结构的基础，外国商人和资本家因而成为上海的贵族阶级。

1. 经济越来越不景气，因而工厂进行裁员，以免受到损失。

2. 由于道德败坏与贫富不均，因而吸毒与犯罪率不断上升。

三. 每当…，总是…   every time …, （always）

※ 开明的外国人，尤其是我所熟悉的美国人，每当我们谈起上海时，总是紧蹙双眉，摇头叹息。

1. 每当我们谈起他的婚姻，他总是眼圈发红，像要落泪似的。

2. 每当大家聚会，他总要谈他打仗的经验。

四. 彼此 V.   to V. with each other

※ 大家彼此和睦相处，所不同的只是职业而已。

1. 只有彼此合作，才能完成任务。

2. 上海的洋人和买办彼此依赖，掌握了上海的商业发展。

五. 不妨   might as well （mostly a suggestion）

※ 只要你有兴致，你不妨在这里消磨两三个钟头。

1. 假期里没有什么特别的事，你不妨利用这个机会去参观博物馆。

2. 虽然经济课跟你的专业没有关系，你有兴趣的话，不妨选这门课。

六. 除非　　　　　　　　　　　　　　　　　　unless

　※ 除非你自己高兴，你不一定要买书。

　1. 除非你有兴趣，你不必作这个工作。

　2. 我每个周末去运动，除非天气太坏。

七. 要不然　　　　　　　　　　　　　　　　otherwise

　※ 你可以跑到戏院去欣赏名伶唱戏，要不然就到故宫博物院去欣赏
　　历代天才所创造的艺术珍品。

　1. 我们可以去游泳，要不然就去跑步。

　2. 你应该多运动，要不然身体会衰弱。

八. 一再　　　　　　　　　　　　again and again, repeatedly

　※ 政府虽然一再易手，这个可爱的古城还是老样子。

　1. 我虽然一再提醒他，他还是忘了。

　2. 中国的国都一再改变，北京仍然是人们最爱的古城。

九. 固然…，却…　　　　　　　it is true that …, but …

　※ 北京的人固然也憧憬着未来，他们却始终浸淫于旧日的光辉里。

　1. 现代的妇女固然有受教育的机会，但无论学校或家长对她们的要
　　求却都较低。

　2. 文字固然应该简化，过分的简化却造成辨认的困难。

十. 不免　　　　　　　　　　　　　　　　unavoidably

　※ 你如果在这里住得太久，你不免有沉醉于西湖的危险。

　1. 他今天又迟到了，老师不免有一点不高兴。

　2. 四散的家人都团聚在一起，父亲特别兴奋，不免多喝了几杯。

（十五）

中國近代思想史上的激進與保守

激進	激进	jījìn	radical
週年	周年	zhōunián	anniversary
講座	讲座	jiǎngzuò	series of lectures
意識	意识	yìshí	consciousness
有意識	有意识	yǒu yìshí	consciously
涉及		shèjí	to mention in passing, to touch upon
現實	现实	xiànshí	reality
特定		tèdìng	specific
傾向	倾向	qīngxiàng	tendency
定點	定点	dìngdiǎn	point of reference
座標	座标	zuòbiāo	(in math) coordinates
極端	极端	jíduān	extreme
激烈		jīliè	violent, radical
摧毀		cuīhuǐ	to destroy, to demolish
現存	现存	xiàncún	existing

秩序		zhìxù	order
概念		gàiniàn	concept, notion
鴉片戰爭	鸦片战争	Yāpiàn zhànzhēng	the Opium War (Britain's invasion of China, 1840-1842)
太平天國	太平天国	Tàipíngtiānguó	the Taiping Heavenly Kingdom (1851-1864), established by Hong Xiuquan during the Taiping Revolution, the largest peasant uprising in China's history
末葉	末叶	mòyè	last years (of a century or dynasty)
穩定	稳定	wěndìng	stable
衡量		héngliáng	to measure, to weigh
特色		tèsè	characteristic
階段	阶段	jiēduàn	stage, phase
魏源		Wèiyuán	Wei Yuan (1794-1856), a famous scholar of the Chin Dynasty
師夷之長技以制夷 师夷之长技以制夷		shī yí zhī cháng jì yǐ zhì yí	to emulate and use the technologies of foreigners to subdue them
口號	口号	kǒuhào	slogan
長處	长处	chángchù	strong points
船堅炮利	船坚炮利	chuán jiān pào lì	the ships are rugged and the artillery is powerful
康有爲	康有为	Kāng Yǒuwéi	Kang Youwei (1858-1927), a scholar who advocated political reform during the reign of Emperor Guangxu of the Qing Dynasty

235

梁啓超	梁启超	Liáng Qǐchāo	Liang Qichao (1873-1929), one of the major advocates of political reform in China in the late 19th century
戊戌變法	戊戌变法	Wùxū biànfǎ	Wu Xu Coup(1898), Kang Youwei and other progressives tried in vain to introduce political reform in China during this coup
對壘	对垒	duìlěi	to be pitted against each other
-氏		shì	a character placed after a family name as a means of address in writing
枝枝節節	枝枝节节	zhīzhījiéjié	branches and knots; minor matters
懷疑	怀疑	huáiyí	to doubt, to suspect
列強		lièqiáng	big powers
瓜分		guāfēn	to carve up, to divide up
危急		wēijí	critical, desperate
情勢	情势	qíngshì	situation
君主立憲	君主立宪	jūnzhǔlìxiàn	constitutional monarchy
不可以道里計		bù kě yǐ dào lǐ jì	immeasurable (by existing standards); extreme
反響	反响	fǎnxiǎng	repercussion, echo
倫理	伦理	lúnlǐ	ethics, moral principles
孔教		Kǒngjiào	Confucianism
創	创	chuàng	to create

仿照		fǎngzhào	to imitate, to follow
接觸	接触	jiēchù	to come into contact with
層面	层面	céngmiàn	layer, stratum
對峙	对峙	duìzhì	confrontation
股		gǔ	measure word used for strength
拼命		pīnmìng	with all one's might, desperately
移用		yíyòng	to shift to
遲疑	迟疑	chíyí	to hesitate, to be hesitant about
反動	反动	fǎndòng	reactionary
退後	退后	tuìhòu	to move back, to regress
平衡		pínghéng	balance, equilibrium
可恥		kěchǐ	shameful, disgraceful
留戀	留恋	liúliàn	to be reluctant to leave (a place) or to part (from somebody)
抱歉		bàoqiàn	to be sorry, to be apologetic
所在		suǒzài	where ...is /lies, location
不成比例		bùchéngbǐlì	to be disproportional
制衡		zhìhéng	to maintain the balance of power

啓蒙運動	启蒙运动	Qǐméng yùndòng	the Enlightenment, a philosophic movement of the 18th century marked by a rejection of traditional social, religious, and political ideas and an emphasis on rationalism
推翻		tuīfān	to overthrow, to overturn
取代		qǔdài	to replace
真理		zhēnlǐ	truth
主體	主体	zhǔtǐ	main component, principal part
壓制	压制	yāzhì	to suppress
混亂	混乱	hùnluàn	chaotic
認同	认同	rèntóng	acceptance; to acclimate to and accept
分家		fēnjiā	to break up the family and live apart; to break with
軌道	轨道	guǐdào	track, course, path
飛馳	飞驰	fēichí	to sprint
第一流		dìyīliú	first- class; the best
強調	强调	qiángdiào	to emphasize
個性	个性	gèxìng	personality, character
解放		jiěfàng	emancipation; to emancipate
一度		yídù	to have v-ed in the past for a period of time

擋不過	挡不过	dǎngbuguò	to be incapable of blocking, hindering, impeding, or stopping
危機	危机	wēijī	crisis
動力	动力	dònglì	motivating force
民族主義	民族主义	mínzúzhǔyì	nationalism
情緒	情绪	qíngxù	morale, mood, feeling
到家		dàojiā	to be perfected; to reach a very high level
支持		zhīchí	to support
承認	承认	chéngrèn	to admit, to recognize
忽視	忽视	hūshì	to neglect, to ignore
大行其道		dà xíng qí dào	to be widely adopted
不惜		bùxī	to not hesitate (to do something)
犧牲	牺牲	xīshēng	to sacrifice
孫中山	孙中山	Sūn Zhōngshān	Dr. Sun Yat-sen (1866 - 1925), father of the Republic of China
中產階級	中产阶级	zhōngchǎnjiējí	middle class
取信於人	取信于人	qǔ xìn yú rén	to gain the confidence of the people
抗戰	抗战	Kàngzhàn	the War of Resistance Against Japan (1937-1945)
主流		zhǔliú	mainstream

阻礙	阻碍	zǔ'ài	to block; obstacle
基調	基调	jīdiào	keynote; basis
馬克思主義	马克思主义	Mǎkèsīzhǔyì	Marxism
五階段論	五阶段论	Wǔjiēduànlùn	按馬克思的看法，人類社會的發展有五個階段：原始共產社會，奴隸社會，封建社會，資本主義社會，共產社會
法則	法则	fǎzé	rule, law
萌芽		méngyá	to sprout, to bud
殖民地		zhímíndì	colony
模式		móshì	pattern, model
缺乏		quēfá	to be short of, to lack
超越		chāoyuè	to surpass, to exceed
不顧	不顾	búgù	to disregard
精華	精华	jīnghuá	essence, cream
資産階級	资产阶级	zīchǎnjiējí	bourgeois class
過程	过程	guòchéng	process, course
否定		fǒudìng	to negate, to deny
負面	负面	fùmiàn	negative

全盤	全盘	quánpán	overall, comprehensive
信仰		xìnyǎng	belief
舉國	举国	jǔguó	the whole nation
思潮		sīcháo	trend of thought, ideological trend
激動	激动	jīdòng	to excite, to stir
參戰	参战	cānzhàn	to enter a war, to take part in a war
渡過	渡过	dùguò	to pass (difficulty), to pull through
爭論	争论	zhēnglùn	to argue; argument
主題	主题	zhǔtí	theme, subject
趨勢	趋势	qūshì	trend, tendency
停頓	停顿	tíngdùn	to stop, to pause
抬頭	抬头	táitóu	to raise one's head; to become a force to be reckoned with
吸引力		xīyǐnlì	appeal, attraction
大聲疾呼	大声疾呼	dàshēng jíhū	to loudly appeal to the public
正視	正视	zhèngshì	to face squarely, to look squarely at
招來	招来	zhāolái	to attract, to court
譏笑	讥笑	jīxiào	to sneer, to ridicule

激起		jīqǐ	to arouse, to stimulate
深思		shēnsī	contemplation
洗禮	洗礼	xǐlǐ	severe test; baptism
理念		lǐniàn	concept, philosophy (of life)
銷路	销路	xiāolù	sale; market
濃厚	浓厚	nónghòu	dense, thick, strong
拒多迎少		jù duō yíng shǎo	much rejection and little acceptance
普及		pǔjí	popular; to popularize
史達林	史达林	Shǐdálín	Joseph V. Stalin (1879-1953)
蘇聯	苏联	Sūlián	the Soviet Union
廢除	废除	fèichú	to abolish
消滅	消灭	xiāomiè	to eliminate, to abolish
私有財產	私有财产	sīyǒucáichǎn	private property
宗族		zōngzú	patriarchal clan
行會	行会	hánghùi	guild (archaic)
同鄉	同乡	tóngxiāng	a person from the same village, town or province
依據	依据	yījù	basis, foundation

名存實亡	名存实亡	míng cún shí wáng	to cease to exist except in name
中央		zhōngyāng	central (government)
伸展		shēnzhǎn	to stretch, to extend
結構	结构	jiégòu	structure
角度		jiǎodù	angle, point of view
天翻地覆		tiān fān dì fù	heaven and earth turning upside down, tremendous
經歷	经历	jīnglì	to experience, to undergo
動亂	动乱	dòngluàn	turmoil, upheaval
對象	对象	duìxiàng	object, target
歷程	历程	lìchéng	course
持續	持续	chíxù	to continue, to sustain
毛澤東	毛泽东	Máozédōng	Mao Zedong (1893-1976)
邊緣	边缘	biānyuán	edge, brink, verge
邊緣性	边缘性	biānyuánxìng	marginal
時機	时机	shíjī	an opportune moment
拋棄	抛弃	pāoqì	to abandon
土改		tǔgǎi	土地改革, land reform

農業合作化	农业合作化	nóngyè hézuòhuà	agricultural collectivization in the 1950s
甘心		gānxīn	to be content with
人民公社		rénmín gōngshè	people's commune
大躍進	大跃进	Dàyuèjìn	the Great Leap Forward, a drive to increase industrial and agricultural production in the late 1950s based on anti-conservatism, anti-waste and self-reliant economic development (generally conceded to be a failure)
空前		kōngqián	unprecedented
災害	灾害	zāihài	calamity, disaster
退却		tuìquè	to retreat
天真		tiānzhēn	innocent, naive
歸因於	归因于	guīyīnyú	to attribute to
無數	无数	wúshù	numerous
因素		yīnsù	factor, element
獲得	获得	huòdé	to gain, to obtain
解釋	解释	jiěshì	to explain; explanation
崩潰	崩溃	bēngkuì	to collapse, to fall apart
止境		zhǐjìng	end, limit
陷入		xiànrù	to fall into, to be caught in

惡性循環	惡性循环	èxìngxúnhuán	vicious cycle
滋生		zīshēng	to cause, to provoke
動盪	动荡	dòngdàng	unrest, turbulence
動機	动机	dòngjī	motive, intention
理直氣壯	理直气壮	lǐzhíqìzhuàng	with justice one one's side, one is bold and assured
煽動	煽动	shāndòng	to instigate, to stir up
群衆	群众	qúnzhòng	the masses
憑藉	凭借	píngjiè	to rely on, to depend on
衝力	冲力	chōnglì	impulsive force, momentum
心聲	心声	xīnshēng	heartfelt wishes, aspirations
百家爭鳴	百家争鸣	bǎi jiā zhēng míng	all schools of thought contend for attention
百花齊放	百花齐放	bǎi huā qí fàng	all flowers are in bloom
氣象	气象	qìxiàng	atmosphere; scene
單調	单调	dāndiào	monotonous
直線	直线	zhíxiàn	straight line
倒轉	倒转	dàozhuǎn	to turn the other way around
方向		fāngxiàng	direction

起點	起点	qǐdiǎn	starting point
不妨		bùfáng	there is no harm in...; might as well
循環圈	循环圈	xúnhuánquān	a cycle
再度		zàidù	once more
中心價值	中心价值	zhōngxīnjiàzhí	central value
譴責	谴责	qiǎnzé	to condemn; to denounce
擁抱	拥抱	yōngbào	to embrace; to hug
主調	主调	zhǔdiào	major emphasis
實質	实质	shízhì	substance; essence
端		duān	end; extremity
轉化	转化	zhuǎnhuà	to change, to transform
強烈		qiángliè	strong, intense, violent
自我意識	自我意识	zìwǒyìshí	self-realization
名教		míngjiào	Confucian etiquette
反抗		fǎnkàng	to resist; resistance
日深		rìshēn	to become deeper day by day
淹沒		yānmò	to submerge, to flood

聯繫	联系	liánxì	contact, connection
合流		héliú	to collaborate, to work hand in glove with
出發	出发	chūfā	to set out, to start off
有過之而無不及 有过之而无不及		yǒu guò zhī ér wú bù jí	to go even farther than in every way
批判		pīpàn	to criticize
薰陶		xūntáo	to exert a gradual, uplifting influence on; to nurture
親切	亲切	qīnqiè	intimate
體驗	体验	tǐyàn	to learn through personal experience
道統	道统	dàotǒng	Confucian orthodoxy
規範	规范	guīfàn	standard, norm
情操		qíngcāo	sentiment
立身處世	立身处世	lì shēn chǔ shì	to establish oneself and manage in the world
約束	约束	yuēshù	to restrain, to keep within bounds
集權體制	集权体制	jíquán tǐzhì	a system of centralizing state power
翻版		fānbǎn	reprint, reproduction
心態	心态	xīntài	way of thinking
相成		xiāngchéng	to complement each other

長程	长程	chángchéng	in the long run
挑戰	挑战	tiǎozhàn	challenge
大幅度		dàfúdù	large scale
絲毫	丝毫	sīháo	the slightest amount or degree
決裂		juéliè	to break with
一味		yíwèi	blindly
客觀	客观	kèguān	objective
冷靜		lěngjìng	sober, calm
無緣	无缘	wúyuán	no opportunity or chance
人文		rénwén	the humanities
衰落		shuāiluò	to decline, to be on the wane
驚人	惊人	jīngrén	astonishing, amazing
猛烈		měngliè	fierce, vigorous
糟粕		zāopò	dregs
取其精華去其糟粕 取其精华去其糟粕		qǔ qí jīnghuá qù qí zāopò	to take the best and discard the worst, to gather the grains and discard the husks
門面話	门面话	ménmiànhuà	formal and insincere remarks
藉口	借口	jièkǒu	an excuse

矯枉過正	矫枉过正	jiǎowǎng guòzhèng	to exceed the proper limits in righting a wrong, to overcorrect
代價	代价	dàijià	price, cost
教訓	教训	jiàoxùn	lesson, moral
黨同伐異	党同伐异	dǎng tóng fá yì	to defend those who belong to one's own faction and attack those who don't, be narrowly partisan
言之成理		yán zhī chéng lǐ	to sound reasonable, to speak in a rational and convincing way
持之有故		chí zhī yǒu gù	to have sufficient grounds for one's views
容忍		róngrěn	to tolerate
高漲	高涨	gāozhǎng	to rise, to upsurge
雅量		yǎliàng	magnanimity, generosity
動輒	动辄	dòngzhé	frequently, at every turn
輕薄	轻薄	qīngbó	disrespectful, irreverent
敵視	敌视	díshì	to be hostile to
一系列		yíxìliè	a series of
結論	结论	jiélùn	conclusion

中国近代思想史上的激进与保守

词语例句

一．无论如何   no matter what

　※ …无论如何，这两个态度是相对于某一种现存的秩序来说的。

　1．无论如何，你一定得帮我这个忙，这件事对我太重要了。

　2．我跟他谈了很久，但他无论如何不同意我的意见。

二．极其 adj.   to be extremely adj.

　※ 这种思想激进得不可以道里计，所以引起的反响也极其巨大。

　1．美国近几年非法移民的问题极其严重。

　2．他的看法极其激进，一般人简直无法接受。

三．为…而…   to V. for the sake of

　※ 求知是一种很高的价值，是一种为知识而知识的态度，为求真理
　　 而求真理的态度。

　1．我并不是为我自己而这么主张，我是为了大家的利益。

　2．为国家而牺牲生命是极其伟大的。

四．一度   once, on one occasion

　※ 在中国五四前后的几年，个性解放一度提出，个人主义也一度出
　　 现。

　1．他一度想设立一所学校，可是没有成功。

　2．中国一些知识分子一度提倡世界语，希望全世界的人能用同一种语
　　 言互相沟通。

五．不惜   not begrudge（in doing something）

　※ 为了民族的生存，我们不惜牺牲个人的自由，来完成民族的自由。

　1．为了作好研究，他不惜整个假期都留在实验室里。

2. 有人为了事业不惜牺牲家庭的幸福，我是做不到的。

六. 以…而言　　　　　　　　　　　　　as far as … is concerned

※ 以主流的思想界而言，他们大致都认定中国文化是阻碍现代化的。

1. 以中国的乡下人而言，西方的个人主义是相当难以理解的东西。

2. 以现阶段的现代化而言，民主的观念还没有深入人民的生活之中。

七. 不过…而已　　　　　　　　　　　　merely, no more than

※ 这个思想的激进化仍是同一历史趋势的继续发展，不过因为民族
危机而一度停顿而已。

1. 他所说的不过是他的主张而已，并不代表全体的意见。

2. 在许多人的眼中，所谓的现代化不过是西化而已。

八. 以至　　　　　　　　　　　　　　even; with the result that

※ 中国社会只有一个党的组织系统，从中央一直伸展到每一个家庭，
以至个人。

1. 他的成绩太差，而且学习态度也太坏，以至学校把他开除了。

2. 农村的教育太落后，卫生条件也很差，以至死亡率偏高。

九. 就…而言　　　　　　　　　　　　as far as … is concerned

※ 就其中表现的主要倾向而言，我们觉得激进化的历程仍未终止。

1. 就经济发展而言，沿海地区可以说是全国之冠。

2. 就我所了解的情况而言，他们从未放弃对民主与自由的追求。

十. 不妨　　　　　　　　　　might as well（mostly a suggestion）

※ 我们不妨说，经过了七十年的激进化，中国思想史走完了第一个
循环圈，现在又回到了"五四"的起点。

1. 你有空的时候，不妨多到图书馆去看看。

2. 既然你对文学有兴趣，你不妨去听听文学史的课。

十一. A 较之 B   when comparing A to B
※ 第二循环的激进较之第一循环只有过之而无不及。
1. 现代知识分子对社会的责任感较之古人并无差别。
2. 学习语言较之学习语言学，是不同的两件事。

十二. 多少 V. 一点   more or less
※ 传统的规范和情操对他们的立身处世多少还有一些约束作用。
1. 现代社会的人多少都受一点传统的影响。
2. 他既然向你请教，你多少得给他一点指导。

十三. 丝毫   （ not … ） even a little bit
※ 文化上的保守力量几乎丝毫没有发生制衡的作用。
1. 他丝毫不了解我的想法。
2. 他的作品丝毫没有受到西方的影响。

十四. adj. 到…的地步   （ serious or severe ） to … degree
※ 中国人文传统的研究到今天已衰落到惊人的地步。
1. 中国文学的西化到了令人难以相信的地步。
2. 城里交通的混乱到了行人无法过街的地步。

十五. 动辄   easily, at every turn
※ 我们是不是能够对于保守的或近乎保守的言论不动辄加以轻薄或
敌视？
1. 西方的评论家动辄批评中国的人口政策，认为侵犯了基本人权，
这完全出于他们对中国现况的不了解。
2. 激进的思想家动辄把中国的落后归因于传统，这种看法并不公平。

生词索引

本索引按汉语拼音字母顺序排列。

各词条后的数目字表示该词条在词汇本中的页数。

bùzhī qísuǒyǐrán 不知其所以然 not knowing why it is so 102

bùzhībùjué 不知不覺 unwittingly 121, 191

bùzhòu 步驟 steps, procedure 203

bùzhì 布置 to decorate 39

bǐ àn 彼岸 the other shore 68

bǐcǐ 彼此 互相 222

bǐngguó 秉國 to dominate a country 189

bǐnǐ 比擬 comparison, metaphor 166

bǐshì 鄙視 to look down upon 68

bì 避 to escape 124

bì'nànsuǒ 避難所 refuge 221

bìbùkěshǎo 必不可少 必須有 198

bìguān zìshǒu 閉關自守 to close the country to international intercourse 135

bìhù 庇護 to protect 222

bìrán 必然 inevitable, certain 2

C

cāiquán 猜拳 to play a Chinese drinking game 12

cān'guān 參觀 to visit, to look around 83

cānghuáng 蒼黃 yellow and pale 87

cānzhàn 參戰 to enter a war, to take part in a war 241

cāochǎng 操場 sports field, playground 56, 81

cāomǐfàn 糙米飯 (cooked) coarse rice, generally eaten by the poor 139

cāozòng 操縱 to exercise (power) 201

cǎi 睬 to pay attention to 39

cǎiqǔ 採取 to adopt 195

cǎizhāi 採摘 to pick 210

cǎnbái 慘白 dreadfully pale 83

cǎnrán 慘然 sadly, sorrowfully 4

cǎntòng 慘痛 painful 190

cǎochuàng 草創 rough to initiate, in the initial stages 112

cáifá 財閥 financial magnate 201

cáifù 財富 wealth 179, 201

cáiliào 材料 ingredient, material 100, 166, 212

cáilì 財力 wealth 218

cáizhèng 財政 finance 117

cáizhì 才智 wisdom and ability 195

cán 蠶 silkworm 104

cánběn 殘本 incomplete copy 120

cáng 藏 to hide 144

cánkù 殘酷 cruel 180

cánkuì 慚愧 to be ashamed 54

Cáoshì 曹氏 Mrs. Cao 115

Cài Jiémín 蔡孑民 蔡元培,(學者,教育家)(1868-1940) 194

càiyuán 菜園 vegetable garden 145

céng 層 layer 12

céngmiàn 層面 layer, stratum 237

chībuxiāo 吃不消 受不了 176

chīfàn 吃飯 to make a living (metaphor) 10

chījīng 吃驚 to be startled, to be shocked 6

chāichú 拆除 to tear down 227

chāo 抄 to copy by hand 104

chāoběn 抄本 handwritten copy 105

chāorén 超人 to be above average, outstanding 195

chāoyuè 超越 to go beyond 201

chāyāng 插秧 to transplant rice seedlings 138

chāyāo 叉腰 to place arms akimbo 13

chāyǐháolí 差以毫厘 (由於)非常小的差別 186

chǎngshāng 廠商 manufacturer and business firms 10

chǎozuǐ 吵嘴 to quarrel 127

cháfěn 搽粉 to powder one's face, to apply makeup 41

cháhú 茶壺 teapot 81

chángchéng 長程 in the long run 248

chángchóng 長蟲 snake 80

chángchù 長處 strong points 235

chánggōng 長工 long-term hired hand 138

Chángshā 長沙 Changsha city 138

chángshān 長衫 long gown 104

chángtài 常態 normal 11, 158

chángtǒng 長筒 long and tube-shaped 79

chánrào 纏繞 entanglement 25

chánsēng 禪僧 Buddhist monk 188

chánzhù 纏住 to entwine 102

cháo 巢 nest 89

cháo 朝 towards 70

cháoliú 潮流 tide, trend, tendency 163, 214

cháonòng 嘲弄 to mock 169

cháoxiào 嘲笑 to laugh at, to ridicule 68, 205

cháozhe 朝著 toward 193

chàndǒu 顫抖 to shake, to shiver 89

chàngdǎo 倡導 to initiate 166

chànlì 顫慄 to shiver, to tremble 78

chànsuǒ 顫索 to shiver, to tremble 87

chēfū 車夫 driver 55

chēng 稱 to call 108

chēngbīng 稱兵 to set up a military force 202

chēngbà 稱霸 to achieve hegemony 200
chēnghū 稱呼 form of address, title 38
chēngzhīwéi 稱之為 to call it... 203
chéncuì 沉醉 to be intoxicated with 231
chénfēngde 塵封的 dust-covered 26
chéng 盛 to place into (a container) 40
chéngdù 程度 level 121
chéngfá 懲罰 punishment, retribution 28
chéngfèn 成分 elements 187
chéngjiàn 成見 preconceived idea 164
chéngjí 成集 to be collected into a volume 108
chénglì 成立 to be tenable, to be able to stand
up (to an argument) 163
chéngniánrén 成年人 adult 139
chéngrán 誠然 的確 177
chéngrèn 承認 to admit, to recognize 239
chéngshí 誠實 honest 43, 62, 140
chéngxù 程序 procedure 176
chénmèn 沈悶 depressing, oppressive 88
chénmò 沈默 reticent, silent, quiet 19, 57
chénrù 沈入 to sink into 103
chénshè 陳設 furnishings, display 39
chénzhòng 沉重 heavy 29
chénzuì 沉醉 to become intoxicated 69
chèdǐ 徹底 thoroughly, completely 195
chōng 衝 to rush, to charge 86
chōngdǎo 衝倒 to crush 135
chōngfèn 充分 fully 180
chōngjǐng 憧憬 to look forward to 227
chōnglì 衝力 impulsive force, momentum 245
chōngsè 充塞 充滿 225
chōngtū 衝突 conflict 164
chōukòng 抽空 擠出時間 223
chōuyá 抽芽 to bud 82
chóngbài 崇拜 to worship 167, 218
Chóngqìng 重慶 city in Sichuan province 204
chóngshàng 崇尚 to uphold 219
chóuhèn 仇恨 to hate 220
chóurén 仇人 personal enemy 65
chóuróng 愁容 worried look 64
chòng 衝 to direct (one's attack, etc.) toward 6
chòuchóng 臭蟲 bedbug 6
chí zhī yǒugù 持之有故 to have sufficient
grounds for one's views 249
chíhuǎn 遲緩 slow 195
chíxù 持續 to continue, to sustain 243
chíyí 遲疑 to hesitate, to be hesitant about 63,
237
chuī dízi 吹笛子 to play the flute 42

chuāngtái 窗台 windowsill 79
chuānliú bùxí 川流不息 never-ending 218
chuānzī 川資 traveling expenses 95
chuán jiān pào lì 船堅炮利 the ships are
rugged and the artillery is powerful 235
chuǎngjìn 闖進 to run into 55
chuán' gěi 傳給 to pass on 71
chuángyán 床沿 the edge of a bed 66
chuánjiào 傳教 to proselytize 168
chuánrǎn 傳染 to infect 108
chuánshuō 傳說 to be on peoples' lips 141
chuàitián 踹田 to tread the field 138
chuàng 創 to create 236
chuàngshǐ 創始 to found 101
chuàngzào 創造 creation 157, 214, 224
chuàngzuò 創作 to write, to create 161
chuànmén 串門 to visit or gossip from door to
door 80
chuí 垂 to hang down, to let fall 47, 65, 77
chū rén tóu dì 出人頭地 to stand out from
one's fellows 223
chūbǎn 出版 to publish 101
chūfā 出發 to set out, to start off 89, 247
chūhū yìliàozhīwài 出乎意料之外 beyond
expectation 35, 59
chūhū yìliàozhīwài 出乎意料之外 contrary
to one's expectations 149
chūjià 出嫁 (of a woman) to get married 115
chūlì 出力 to exert oneself 152
chūmài 出賣 to sell 45
chūnhuā qiūyuè 春花秋月 spring flower and
autumn moon--the best things at the best times
166
chūshēn 出身 economic, family and class
background 139
chūshén 出神 to be engrossed in meditation, to
be spellbound 25, 145
chūtóu 出頭 to free from (misery) 65
chūyī 初一 the first day of a lunar month 139
chūyú 出於 to stem from 204
chūzǒu 出走 to run away 149
chǔlǐ 處理 to deal with, to handle 49
chǔn 蠢 foolish 38
chǔzài 處在 to be in (a certain condition) 137
chúfēi 除非 unless 57
chúncuì 純粹 pure 160
chúnjìng 純淨 pure and clean 19
chúxī 除夕 New Year's Eve 124
chùdòng 觸動 to stir up 216

258

dàirén shòuzuì 代人受罪 to suffer for the crime of another 68

dàlù 大陸 mainland 190

dàlǐshí 大理石 marble 78

dàng 當 to pawn, to hock 44, 123

dàngyàng 蕩漾 to rise and fall, ripple, undulate 70

dàngyàng 蕩漾 to wave, to ripple 25

dànmòsè 淡墨色 light ink color 24

dànshēng 誕生 to be born 135

Dànshuǐhé 淡水河 Dan-Shui River 13

dànxīzhījiān 旦夕之間 早晚之間 (表示時間很短) 229

dànyuàn 但願 if only, I wish 5

dànzi 擔子 burden, load 164

dào 倒 to dump 14

dào 道 measure word for a dish in a meal 48

dào 稻 paddy (rice) 211

dàobá 倒拔 to pull up 83

dàodé 道德 morality 188

dàogǔ 稻穀 paddy 141

dàojiā 到家 to be perfected 239

dàotǒng 道統 Confucian orthodoxy 247

dàotóulái 到頭來 in the end, finally 165

dàozhuǎn 倒轉 to turn the other way around 245

dàpào 大炮 artillery 135

dàrǎng 大嚷 to shout loudly 105

dàrénlǎoyé 大人老爺 people of importance, rich VIPs 45

dàshēng jíhū 大聲疾呼 loudly appeal to the public 165

dàshēng jíhū 大聲疾呼 to loudly appeal to the public 241

dàtīng 大廳 front hall 124

dàxíng qídào 大行其道 to be widely adopted 239

dàxìng 大幸 great good fortune 191

Dàyuèjìn 大躍進 the Great Leap Forward, a drive to increase industrial and agricultural production in the late 1950s based on anti-conservatism, anti-waste and self-reliant economic development (generally conceded to be a failure) 244

dàyì 大意 general idea 178

dàzáyuàn 大雜院 a compound occupied by many households 19

dàzhì 大致 more or less 210

dēnglóng 燈籠 lantern 124

dēngtái 登台 to take the stage and perform 45

děng 等 measure word for classified or graded things/people 216

Déchuānshì 德川氏 a shogun in Japanese history (1603-1867) 188

déshèng 得勝 triumphant 7

déxìng 德性 moral conduct 140

déyì 得意 to be proud of oneself 34, 54

dézuì 得罪 to offend 117

dèngzi 凳子 stool 43

diǎnmíng 點名 to take attendance 77

diǎntóng chéngyín 點銅成銀 to turn copper into silver by touching it 215

diǎnyín chéngjīn 點銀成金 to turn silver into gold by touching it 216

diǎnzhuì 點綴 decoration to, embellish 24, 35

diànhù 佃戶 tenant peasant 142

diànlǎn 電纜 cable 16

diào 調 to transfer 112

diàodù 調度 to adjust 123

diàoguòtóu 掉過頭 to turn around 36

diàosǐ 吊死 to hang by the neck 62

diàotóu 掉頭 to turn away 57

diàoyú 釣魚 to fish 15

diàozi 調子 melody 43

diànhuǒ 店夥 shop assistant 223

diēdǎo 跌倒 to fall 55

diēdie 爹爹 daddy 64

diézi 碟子 saucer 40

diū 丟 to lose 44

diū 丟 to throw 14

diūliǎn 丟臉 to make somebody ashamed 122

Dōngjīng 東京 Tokyo 99

dōngjì 冬季 winter 23

dōuquānzi 兜圈子 to go around in circles 149

dǒngshì 懂事 sensible 125

dǒu 抖 to shake, to shiver, to tremble 47, 84, 88

dòng 凍 to freeze 142

dòngdàng 動蕩 unrest, turbulence 245

dòngjī 動機 motive, intention 245

dòngluàn 動亂 turmoil, upheaval 201, 243

dònglì 動力 motive force 239

dòngmài 動脈 artery 218

dòngmù 凍木 to be frozen stiff, numb with cold 87

dòngrénxīnxián 動人心弦 to tug at one's heart strings 224

dòngshǒu 動手 to start work 6

dòngwù 動物 animal 218

dòngzhé 動輒 frequently, at every turn 249

dòushì 鬥士 warrior 197

dòuzhēng 鬥爭 to struggle 148

dòuzi 豆子 bean 80

dí 敵 to match 27

díshì 敵視 to be hostile to 249

duījī 堆積 to store up 26

duān 端 end 246

duān 端 to carry, to hold level with both hands 86

duānzhèng 端正 good-looking 67

duǎn'ǎo 短襖 short Chinese-style jacket 42

duǎngōng 短工 short-term hired hand 139

duǎnpiān xiǎoshuō 短篇小說 short story 108

duànjué 斷絕 to break 28

duànluò 段落 paragraph, convenient stopping point 98

duànsòng 斷送 to ruin 64

duōshǎo 多少 more or less 65

duōyú 多餘 extra, surplus 98

duōyú 多餘 unnecessary 85

duǒ 躲 to hide (oneself) 19,64, 78

duózǒu 奪走 to snatch away 49

duò 墮 to fall, to sink 28

dūdǎo 督導 to supervise and direct 194

dūshì 都市 大城市, metropolis 210

dǔbó 賭博 to gamble 123

dǔzhòu 賭咒 to take an oath 63

dúcái 獨裁 dictatorship 153

dúcái 獨裁 to rule autocratically 195

dúlì zìzhǔ 獨立自主 to be independent and act on one's own 136

dúshé 毒蛇 poisonous snake 102

dúsù 毒素 poison 17

dúwǔ 黷武 militaristic 198

dúzì 獨自 alone 128

dùguò 渡過 to pass (difficulty), to pull through 241

dùjí 妒嫉 jealousy 59

dùjì 妒忌 to be jealous of 35

dùliàng 度量 tolerance, capacity for forgiveness 205

Dùlǔmén 杜魯門 Harry S. Truman (1884-1972) 179

dùnzhòng 鈍重 blunt, bluntly 79

duìkàng 對抗 to oppose 153

duìlěi 對壘 to be pitted against each other 236

duìxiàng 對象 target, object 10, 243

duìyú 對於 to, for 143, 214

duìzhì 對峙 confrontation 237

dǐdá 抵達 到達 186

dǐkàng 抵抗 resistance 148

dǐkàng 抵抗 to resist 69

dìbǎn 地板 floor 77

dìdū 帝都 capital of an empire 209

dìguózhǔyì 帝國主義 imperialism 134, 165

dìlǐ 地理 geography 78

dìngdiǎn 定點 point of reference 234

dìnglì 訂立 to sign into effect 135

dìngqīn 定親 to get engaged 88

dìngshén 定神 to pull oneself together 55

dìtú 地圖 map 89

dìwángjiàngxiàng 帝王將相 emperors, generals, and prime ministers 145

dìwèi 地位 position 215

dìxiàshì 地下室 basement, cellar 87

dìyīliú 第一流 first- class 238

dìzào 締造 to create 195

dìzhèn 地震 earthquake 231

E

ēn 恩 favor 60

ēndiǎn 恩典 favour 63

ēnshī 恩師 benefactor 122

ěxīn 惡心 to feel sick 10

é 鵝 goose 225

érbèi 兒輩 children 141

érkuàng 而況 moreover 96

èchòu 惡臭 foul smelling 14

èdú 惡毒 vicious 69

Eguó 俄國 Russia 177

èliè 惡劣 odious, abominable 159

èryí 二姨 second aunt 80

èshā 扼殺 to strangle in the cradle 18

èxìngxúnhuán 惡性循環 vicious cycle 245

F

fā láosāo 發牢騷 to grumble 127

fācái 發財 to get rich, to make a fortune 1

fācíbēi 發慈悲 to show mercy 66

fādǒu 發抖 to shiver, to shake 142

fādòng 發動 to launch 191

fāduān 發端 to originate, to start 97

fāhóng 發紅 to turn red 5

264

268

271

lùnzhǎngyòu 論長幼 as far as age is concerned 27

lùxiàn 路線 route 193

lǜzhōu 綠洲 oasis 221

lǐjiào 禮教 the Confucian ethical code 166

Lǐjì 禮記 The Book of Rites 118

Lǐkuí 李逵 a character in The Water Margin 120

lǐlùn 理論 theory 148, 163

lǐlùn 理論 講道理 15

lǐngdǎo 領導 to lead 158

lǐngkǒu 領口 collarband, neckband 83

lǐngtǔ 領土 territory 136

lǐngwù 領悟 to comprehend 158

lǐngxiù 領袖 leader 158, 193

lǐniàn 理念 concept, philosophy (of life) 242

lǐzhíqìzhuàng 理直氣壯 with justice one one's side, one is bold and assured 245

lǐzhì 理智 reason, intellect 158

lì shēn chǔ shì 立身處世 to establish oneself and manage in the world 247

lìchǎng 立場 standpoint 163

lìchéng 歷程 course 243

lìdài 歷代 past dynasties/ages 209, 224

lìfǎ wěiyuán 立法委員 member of the legislature 18

lìguó 立國 to establish a country 191

lìjīng 歷經 to undergo 187

lìlùn 立論 to take a stand 1

lìngxíng 另行另外 196

lìqiú 力求 努力追求 219

lìwài 例外 exception 148

lìyòng 利用 to use 222

lìzài 立在 to stand at 41

M

māde 媽的 Damn! 80

mǎchēfū 馬車夫 carriage driver 84

mǎibàn 買辦 comprador 215

Mǎkèsī 馬克思 Karl Marx (1818-1883) 175

Mǎkèsīzhǔyì 馬克思主義 Marxism 240

Mǎlìyà 馬利亞 transliteration of Maria 87

mǎn...suì 滿...歲 to be...a full years old 115

mǎnxīn 滿心 to...with all one's heart 46

mǎnyuè 滿月 a baby's completion of its first month of life 1

mǎnzú 滿足 satisfaction 27

mǎyǐ 螞蟻 ant 220

mái 埋 to bend over 37

máixiàtóu 埋下頭 to immerse oneself into 58

mámù 麻木 numb 99

mán 瞞 to hide (the truth) 27

mán 鰻 eel 211

mánbùliǎo 瞞不了騙不了 175

mángmánglùlù 忙忙碌碌 忙 220

mángrán 茫然 blankly 46

mántou 饅頭 steamed bun 44, 78

mányě 蠻野 wild, uncivilized 83

máodùn 矛盾 contradiction 153, 165, 192

máokēng 茅坑 latrine pit 18

Máozédōng 毛澤東 Mao Zedong (1893-1976) 131, 243

mázíliǎn 麻子臉 a pockmarked face 78

mázuì 麻醉 to numb 103

mà 罵 to scold 7

màoqì 冒氣 to emit vapor, to steam 81

měi 每 often 195

měidāng 每當 whenever 217

měidé 美德 moral excellence 141, 193

měiféng 每逢 everytime when 79, 140

měimǎn 美滿 happy, wonderful 97

měishù 美術 fine art 100

měngliè 猛烈 fierce, vigorous 248

měngshì 猛士 brave warrior 107

méi chūxi 没出息 good-for-nothing 25

méifèn 没份 to not have a share 5

méimao 眉毛 eyebrow 37

méng 蒙 to be subjected to 151

méngguǎn 蒙館 old style private school 118

méngyá 萌芽 to sprout, to bud 240

méngzhe... demíng 蒙著...的名 to receive the unmerited title of 108

méngzhù 蒙住 to cover 67

ménhù kāifàng 門戶開放 open door 203

ménhù 門戶 門 210

ménkǎn 門檻 threshold 114

ménmiànhuà 門面話 formal and insincere remarks 248

mènsǐ 悶死 to die of suffocation 105

miǎnbùliǎo 免不了 to be unable to avoid 115

miǎndé 免得 so as to avoid 61

miǎománg 渺茫 uncertain 116

miǎoshì 藐視 to look down upon 59

miáoshù 描述 to describe 11

miáoxiě 描寫 to describe 165

miànkǒng 面孔 face 34

miànlín 面臨 to confront, to face 136

miànmào 面貌 face 33

miànpáng 面龐 face 140
miànróng 面容 complexion 43
miàochǎn 廟産 temple property 146
mièjué 滅絶 to become extinct 6
miùyǐqiānlǐ 謬以千里 (結果)造成很大的錯誤 186
mōsuǒ 摸索 to grope, to feel about 88
mǒ 抹 to wipe, to wipe away 83
mǒshā 抹殺 to blot out, to write off 106
mǒshā 抹煞 to erase 175
mó 磨 to grind 4
mófǎng 模仿 to imitate 89, 192
móhúbùqīng 模糊不清 vague, unclear 87
móshì 模式 pattern, model 240
móu 謀 to seek 71, 158
móyàng 模樣 appearance 24
mò míng qí miào 莫名其妙 to be baffled 143
mòrì 末日 doomsday 70
mòmòde 黙黙地 silently 47, 64
mòmǐ 磨米 to grind rice 138
mòrú 莫如 nothing is more ... than 126
mòshì 漠視 to ignore 179
Mòsuǒlǐní 墨索里尼 Benito Mussolini (1883-1945) 176
mòwěi 末尾 end 80
Mòxīgē 墨西哥 Mexico 78
mòyè 末葉 last years (of a century or dynasty) 235
mí 迷 to blur 63
míbǔ 彌補 to make up 192
mímàn 彌漫 to fill the air, to spread all over the place 90
míng cún shí wáng 名存實亡 to cease to exist except in name 243
míngcí 名詞 term, phrase 163
míngjiǎo 名角 famous actor or actress 45
míngjiào 名教 Confucian etiquette 246
míngliàng 明亮 bright 17, 39
mínglíng 名伶 famous stage performers 224
Míngmò 明末 the last period of the Ming Dynasty 188
míngmù 名目 title 100
míngshènggǔjī 名勝古跡 scenic spots and historical sites 225
mínguó 民國 中華民國 222
míngyù 名譽 reputation 18
Míngzhìwéixīn 明治維新 Japan's Meiji period (1868-1912) 188
mínjiān 民間 老百姓中間 188

mínzhòng 民眾 the masses 205
mínzúzhǔyì 民族主義 nationalism 239
míxìn 迷信 superstition 146, 206
míyàngde 謎樣的 enigmatic 213
mǔ 畝 a unit of area (=0.0667 hectares) 133
múyàng 模樣 appearance, look 106
mù 幕 an act of a play 190
mùbǎn 木版 wood block (for printing) 96
mùbiāo 目標 objective, target 160
mùdǔ 目睹 親眼看見 157
mùshī 牧師 minister 168
mǐn 敏 keen, sharp 158
mǐtūchǐ 米突尺 the metric ruler 135
mì 密 dense, thick 104
mìmì 秘密 secret 26
mìnglìng 命令 to command 151
mìngyùn 命運 fate 50, 164
mìqiè 密切 close, intimate 140, 166

N

Nanking, 南京 95
nǎozi 腦子 brain 16, 146
ná...kāixīn 拿...開心 to enjoy oneself at other's expense 67
nánnán 喃喃 to mutter 65
Nánsòng 南宋 the Southern Song Dynasty (1127-1279) 187
nánxiōngnándì 難兄難弟 two of a kind, birds of a feather 220
nàhǎn 吶喊 to shout loudly, to cry out 93, 168
nàixīn 耐心 patience 119
nàliáng 納涼 to enjoy the cool (in the open air) 72
nào yìjiàn 鬧意見 to be on bad terms because of differing opinions, to bicker 125
nèidì 內地 inland, interior 137
nèn 嫩 light 24
niǎnsǐ 輾死 to flatten to death 71
niányèfàn 年夜飯 New Year's Eve dinner 124
nóngfù 農婦 peasant woman 141
nónghòu 濃厚 dense, thick, strong 242
nóngjiāzǐ 農家子 a farmer's son 139
nóngliè 濃烈 thick and strong 161
nóngmáng 農忙 busy season (in farming) 138
nóngyè hézuòhuà 農業合作化 agricultural collectivization in the 1950s 244
ní 泥 mud 90
níng 擰 to pinch 123

R

S

shěnmǔ 嬸母 aunt (wife of father's younger brother) 33

shéngmò 繩墨 (carpenter's) marking line 161

shénqíng 神情 facial expression 99

shénqì 神氣 facial expression 59

shénshèng 神聖 sacred, holy 116, 157

shétou 舌頭 tongue 86

shè 射 to shoot (eyesight) 59

shèchū 射出 to emit (light, heat, etc.), to shoot 1

shèfǎ 設法 想辦法 61

shèjiān 舍監 dormitory superintendent 85

shèjí 涉及 to mention in passing, to touch upon 234

shèngjǔ 盛舉 magnificent event, worthy undertaking 99

shènglì 勝利 to win 149

shènglì 勝利 victory 27

shèngrén 聖人 sage, wise man 80

shèngxián jūnzǐ 聖賢君子 sages, men of virtue and noble men 145

shèngyú 剩餘 remainder 134

shènrù 滲入 to infiltrate 168

shǒu 守 to keep watch over 44

shǒubì 手臂 arm 17

shǒuduàn 手段 means, measure 168

Shǒuhuàn 守煥 name of a person 120

shǒupà 手帕 handkerchief 47

shǒushì 首飾 jewelry 94

shǒutào 手套 gloves 80

shǒutíxiāng 手提箱 small suitcase 90

shǒuwàn 手腕 wrist 77

shǒuxīn 手心 the palm of the hand 82

shǒuzú 手足 手腳 114

shòu zhémó 受折磨 to suffer 13

shòucháng 瘦長 thin and tall 55

shòuhàirén 受害人 victim 20

shòushāng 受傷 to be injured 11

shòuxíng 受刑 to be put to torture 69

shíchái 拾柴 to collect firewood 141

shíguāng 時光 time 93

shíjī 時機 an opportune moment 160, 243

shíjiē 石階 stone steps 87

shíjié 時節 time, season 23, 141

shíjì yánzhī 實際言之 as a matter of fact 191

shílǎilǐ 十來里 十幾里 149

shíshí 時時 often 38

shíshì 時事 current events 98

shíwù zhòngdú 食物中毒 food poisoning 18

shíwù 什物 雜物 26

shíxià 時下 present, current 161

shíyòng 食用 吃的和用的 134

shízhì 實質 substance 246

shízìjià 十字架 cross 135

shuāiluò 衰落 to decline, to be on the wane 187, 248

shuāng 霜 frost 94

shuāngxī 雙膝 both knees 152

shuǎqián 耍錢 to gamble (archaic), 賭博 5

shuō hǎo shuō dǎi 說好說歹 to say whatever it takes 124

shuōhuǎng 說謊 to lie 2

shuōkè 說客 a persuasive talker 18

shūcài 蔬菜 vegetables 139

shūchàng 舒暢 happy, entirely free from worry 85

shūfù 叔父 uncle 33

Shūjīng 書經 The Book of History 118

shūtǎn 舒坦 to be at ease, to feel comfortable 6

shūtóu 梳頭 to comb hair 41

shūyuǎn 疏遠 to become estranged 71

shǔniú 屬牛 born in the year of the ox 63

shǔyú 屬於 to belong to 119, 167

shú 贖 to redeem 46

shúshuì 熟睡 to sleep soundly 105

shúzì 熟字 words learned 115

shù 豎 to erect, to set upright 81

shùcóng 樹叢 grove, thicket 83

shùmù 數目 amount 54

shùyīn 樹蔭 shade of a tree 145

shùyǔ 術語 terminology 150

shùzhī 樹枝 branch, twig 78

shuǐ shēn huǒ rè 水深火熱 deep water and scorching fire- an abyss of suffering 165

Shuǐhǔzhuàn 水滸傳 The Water Margin by Shi Nai'an 120, 144

shuǐtáng 水塘 pond 151

shǐ 駛 to drive 55

Shǐdálín 史達林 Joseph V. Stalin (1879-1953) 242

shǐmìng 使命 mission 164

shǐwúqiánlì 史無前例 unprecedented 189

shǐzhōng 始終 from beginning to end 117

shì 氏 a character placed after a family name as a means of address in writing 236

shì ruò wú dǔ 視若無睹 to take no notice of what one sees 165

shì 逝 to pass, to pass away 93

X

yāpò 壓迫 to oppress 145

yāsuìqián 壓歲錢 money given to children as a New Year's gift 124

yātou 丫頭 servant girl, slave girl 40

yāyì 壓抑 suppression, oppression 166

yāzhì 壓制 to suppress 238

yǎliàng 雅量 magnanimity, generosity 249

yǎn zhēngzhēngde 眼睜睜地 (looking on) helplessly 45

yǎn 演 to perform 36

yǎngtóu 仰頭 to raise one's head 23

yǎnguāng 眼光 eye, glance , foresight 1, 157

yǎnjiǎo 眼角 the corner of the eye 4, 42

yǎnjìng 眼鏡 glasses, spectacles 1

yǎnquān 眼圈 rim of the eye 5

yǎnzhù 掩住 to cover, to conceal 88

yán zhī chéng lǐ 言之成理 to sound reasonable, to speak in a rational and convincing way 249

yáncháng 延長 to extend 65

yándōng 嚴冬 severe winter 25

yánghuòdiàn 洋貨店 store selling foreign goods 50

yánglǐu 楊柳 willow 24

yángqiāng 洋槍 foreign guns 135

yángshù 楊樹 poplar tree 82

yángwù 洋務 foreign things, foreign business 95

yánliào 顏料 pigment, dye 86

yánlì 嚴厲 strict, stern 122, 147

yáohàn 搖撼 to shake to the foundation 61

yànfán 厭煩 to be fed up with, to be sick of 86

yànwù 厭惡 disgusting 126

yàoyǐn 藥引 an ingredient added to enhance the efficacy of a dose of medicine 94

yàozhuó 要著 important move 100

yěwài 野外 field 144

yōngbào 擁抱 to embrace 246

yōnghù 擁護 to support, to uphold 159

yōuhòu 優厚 munificent 119

yōumò 幽默 humorous 149

yōuxián 悠閑 leisurely 145

yōuxiù 優秀 outstanding, excellent 158

yǒngměng 勇猛 bold and powerful 107

yǒngqì 勇氣 courage 14

yǒngtàn 詠嘆 to utter lofty praises about, to wax eloquent on 162

yǒu guīlǜ de 有規律地 orderly 77

yǒu guò zhī ér wú bù jí 有過之而無不及 to go even farther than in every way 182,247

yǒu yìshí 有意識 consciously 234

yǒugōng 有功 to have rendered great service 7

yǒuyì 有意 intentionally, purposely 97

yǒuzhǒng 有種 to have guts 15

yóu...zìbiàn 由 . . .自便 to do as one pleases 95

yóuwū 油污 greasy dirt 12

yóuxì 游戲 game 28

yóuyán 油鹽 oil and salt 151

yóuyǒng 游泳 to swim 17

yóuyù 猶豫 hesitation 164

yòunián 幼年 childhood 35, 142

yòuzhì 幼稚 puerile, naive 97

yíbìng 一並 together 30

yíchǎn 遺產 property left by the deceased 49

yídòng 移動 to move, to shift 78, 90

yídù 一度 to have v-ed in the past for a period of time 238

yíguàn 一貫 all along, consistently 141

yíjiāo 移交 to turn over to 118

yín fēng nòng yuè 吟風弄月 to sing of the moon and the wind- sentimental verse 165

yín'ěr 銀耳 a kind of semi-transparent white fungus believed to be highly nutritious 5

yínyuán 銀元 silver dollar 118

yítàitài 姨太太 concubine 46

yíwèi 一味 blindly 248

yíxīn 疑心 to doubt 46

yíxīn 疑心 to suspect 167

yíxìliè 一系列 a series of 249

yíyòng 移用 to shift to 237

yízhǔ 遺囑 written will 116

yízhì 一致 identical, consistent 162

yuānkǔ 冤苦 wrongful treatment 5

yuānniè 冤孽 wrong and sin 67

yuānwǎng 冤枉 to wrongfully assign blame 44

yuānwǎng 冤枉 unjust 150

yuánběn 原本 the original text 11

yuánduì 原對 the original pair 94

yuángù 緣故 reason 38

yuánshǐ 原始 primitive 168

yuányóu 緣由 reason, cause 108

yuàn 怨 complaint 30

yuànhèn 怨恨 grudge 29

yuànhèn 怨恨 to have a grudge against somebody 87

CPSIA information can be obtained at www.ICGtesting.com
Printed in the USA
BVOW050144090413

317660BV00003B/7/A